CLOUD-DRIVEN DEFENSE

Integrating Cybersecurity Principles into Scalable IT Cloud Development for Secure Digital Transformation

Mariam Sanusi

Cloud-Driven Defense: Integrating Cybersecurity Principles into Scalable IT Cloud Development for Secure Digital Transformation

Published In Nigeria by:
Emphaloz Publishing House
www.emphaloz.com

Table of Contents

Preface

When I began my journey in IT engineering and cybersecurity, cloud computing was still considered a novelty, an emerging convenience rather than the business-critical necessity it has become today. Over the years, I have watched this technology evolve, not just in capability but in complexity, reach, and risk. Cloud systems now power some of the most sensitive transactions in financial institutions, healthcare networks, and national infrastructures. And yet, despite all the advancements, the question I keep returning to is this: Are we building secure systems, or are we building fast systems we hope will be secure later?

This book was born from that tension.

In my experience working across cloud architecture, automation, and cybersecurity, I've seen firsthand how often security is an afterthought added only after deployment, patched only after a breach. I've also seen how organizations struggle to bridge the communication gap between software developers and security professionals, leaving critical vulnerabilities exposed not by malice but by misunderstanding.

Cloud-Driven Defense is my response to that gap. It is not just a technical manual, though you will find code samples, automation strategies, and security frameworks inside. It is also a call for cultural change for engineers and business leaders alike to embed cybersecurity at the core of every scalable solution.

This book is structured to serve both the practitioner and the decision-maker. Whether you're a security engineer looking to automate threat detection in your CI/CD pipeline, a cloud architect tasked with designing resilient infrastructure, or a business executive trying to understand the security implications of digital transformation, you'll find insights you can apply immediately.

You'll also find stories. Real projects. Real challenges. And real consequences. Because cybersecurity is not a checklist, it's a mindset. It's about anticipating, mitigating, and learning. It's about accountability.

I invite you to read this book not just as a guide, but as a blueprint for secure innovation. We can build scalable systems. We can drive digital transformation. But we must do so with defense in mind by default, not by design flaw.

Foreword

It is no exaggeration to say we are living through one of the most defining shifts in the history of technology. Over the past decade, cloud computing has moved from fringe adoption to foundational infrastructure fueling everything from mobile banking to remote surgery, virtual classrooms to AI research labs. The modern economy is being rebuilt in the cloud. And with this transformation comes a critical responsibility: securing that infrastructure against an evolving spectrum of cyber threats.

Cloud-Driven Defense arrives at a time when that responsibility has never been more urgent.

Cybersecurity in the cloud is not a bolt-on feature or a back-office consideration. It is central to the trust users place in systems, the resilience of business operations, and the integrity of data that fuels everything we now call "digital." Yet despite this reality, many organizations remain unprepared. They build for speed, scale, and convenience often relegating security to a checklist that comes too late, or worse, not at all.

This is what makes Mariam Adetoun Sanusi's work not only timely but essential. In a world overflowing with technical documentation, buzzwords, and high-level frameworks, this book stands apart by doing something rare: it connects the dots between secure cloud engineering, organizational transformation, and practical execution.

Mariam writes not just as a cybersecurity professional, but as someone who has worked at the intersections between developers and security teams, between policy and practice, between business outcomes and technical design. Her experience navigating these spaces gives this book both credibility and clarity.

Across ten structured chapters, Cloud-Driven Defense takes the reader on a journey from foundational cloud principles to real-world case studies involving secure deployments, threat mitigation, automation, and governance. The writing is accessible without being oversimplified, detailed without being overwhelming. Whether you're managing risk in a fintech platform, leading a cloud migration in an enterprise environment, or mentoring graduate students on cloud security practices, this book offers insights that are both immediate and enduring.

One of the most powerful aspects of this work is its emphasis on culture. Mariam does not present security as a mere toolset but as a mindset. She makes the case that true transformation in the cloud space requires a shift in how we think about responsibility, collaboration, and design. Developers must speak the language of security. Security professionals must understand the tempo of agile delivery. And leadership must be willing to fund not just innovation, but secure innovation.

Her chapter on DevSecOps, in particular, demonstrates how shared accountability and automation can lead to more resilient systems without slowing down development. The case studies from her own work are refreshingly candid, showing both successes and hard-learned lessons, and they offer blueprints that teams across industries can adapt to their own unique challenges.

There is also a strong message of empowerment here. This book doesn't preach; it equips. It gives cybersecurity practitioners, cloud architects, and tech leaders the frameworks they need to rethink their assumptions and build better. And for young professionals and graduate students entering the field, it provides an aspirational yet realistic look at what good cloud security practice looks like on the ground.

In a rapidly evolving threat landscape where misconfigurations, privilege escalations, and cloud-native attacks are becoming daily headlines, the need for grounded, tested, and actionable knowledge has never been greater.

If you are serious about building systems that scale and withstand pressure, that innovate and comply, that move fast and stay secure, this book is for you.

Introduction

Cloud computing was once a novelty, an experimental technology reserved for forward-thinking developers and large enterprises willing to take a bet on flexibility over control. At the time, its promises were exciting but unproven. People questioned its reliability, its security, even its legitimacy as a viable infrastructure model. Fast forward a decade, and the conversation has shifted dramatically. Today, cloud systems are not only mainstream, but they are also mission critical.

Entire industries are now built on the cloud. Financial systems run on it. Healthcare data is stored in it. Education, transportation, governance, logistics, every sector you can imagine relies on the invisible network of virtual machines, containers, and services that define our digital age. But somewhere along this path of rapid adoption, an uncomfortable truth has emerged: the speed at which we've embraced the cloud has far outpaced the attention we've given to securing it.

This book exists to confront that reality head-on.

Over the years, I've worked on engineering teams that built elegant solutions on fragile foundations. I've reviewed systems where access controls were an afterthought, credentials were exposed in logs, and critical data passed through unmonitored endpoints. Not because people didn't care but because people were overwhelmed. Budgets are tight. Timelines are tighter.

And too often, security becomes the thing we promise to fix after launch.

But "after" is usually too late.

Cloud-Driven Defense is my way of pulling the brakes, of saying, let's rethink how we build. It is a book born from real projects, real challenges, and real consequences. It doesn't pretend that cloud security is easy, or that every company can afford a state-of-the-art SOC or a team of seasoned threat hunters. What it does offer is something far more attainable: clarity.

It offers clarity on what cloud security really means beyond buzzwords. It offers clarity on how engineers and security professionals can work together without slowing each other down. It offers clarity on why scalable infrastructure and secure design are not mutually exclusive goals but two sides of the same discipline.

This book was not written for theorists. It was written for builders.

For engineers, writing production code. For DevOps teams managing increasingly complex pipelines. For cybersecurity professionals trying to introduce guardrails without being seen as the "no" department. For business leaders who sign off on architecture decisions they don't always understand, but whose consequences they always inherit. For students, too, those preparing to enter the field, eager to contribute but unsure how to connect the dots between development, automation, and defense.

Throughout these chapters, I've included not only frameworks and strategies, but stories. I believe in stories. They stay with us longer than models or acronyms. You'll read about deployments that succeeded and others that nearly collapsed under their own weight. You'll see how automation can be a gift or a curse, depending on how it's handled. You'll learn where missteps often happen, not just because of bad code, but because of misaligned teams, rushed timelines, or unclear accountability.

This is not a book that scolds. It's a book that equips.

My hope is that when you finish it, you'll walk away not just with technical insight, but with a stronger sense of purpose. The cloud is not going anywhere. And neither are the threats. Our job is not to stop building; it is to build better.

Let's begin with defense in mind.

Chapter One

Foundations of Secure Cloud Development

Cloud computing did not arrive with a bang. It slipped in quietly, steadily, first as an experimental infrastructure solution, then as a convenience, and eventually as a business imperative. In its earliest days, cloud systems were regarded with suspicion. IT managers questioned the logic of surrendering control to remote servers. Security professionals raised alarms over data privacy, integrity, and sovereignty. But as use cases multiplied and the benefits became too pronounced to ignore, resistance gave way to rapid adoption. Within a decade, cloud infrastructure became not only acceptable but essential.

Today, it powers everything from core banking systems to social media platforms, government databases to AI pipelines. What once seemed like an abstract concept, "the cloud" is now the most tangible layer of global digital infrastructure. And yet, despite its ubiquity, many organizations continue to approach cloud development with a mindset inherited from on-premise systems where security is often reactive, patchwork, and siloed from core development processes. That approach is no longer viable.

Understanding the foundation of secure cloud development requires looking back at how digital infrastructure has evolved, and at the assumptions that no longer hold true in today's landscape. In the traditional IT setup, security was perimeter-based. Firewalls, antivirus tools, and tightly controlled physical access to servers created a walled fortress around sensitive data. The assumption was simple: keep the bad actors out, and everything inside the network would remain safe. But the cloud breaks that model completely. There is no single "perimeter" anymore. Every API, every container, every endpoint is now its own micro perimeter. The trust boundaries have shifted, and so must the principles that guide our systems.

One of the most important shifts is the recognition that security can no longer be isolated from development. In a cloud-native environment, where infrastructure is coded and deployments happen in minutes, the idea of security as a final checklist is dangerous. You can't secure a system after it's built, you have to secure it as it's being designed, as it's being coded, and as it's being deployed. Security becomes a continuous process, not a one-time approval. It is both cultural and technical.

This reality is often uncomfortable for teams used to traditional separation of duties. Developers want to build fast. Security teams want to build safely. Business executives want to ship. Everyone is under pressure. And so, security becomes the casualty not because it's unimportant, but because it's misunderstood. People still see it as a blocker, rather than a discipline that, when integrated early, actually improves system resilience, reduces long-term costs, and builds user trust.

In my experience, the organizations that thrive in the cloud are not necessarily the ones with the biggest budgets or most advanced tooling. They are the ones that understand this mindset shift. They invest early in cross-functional collaboration. They educate developers on secure design. They involve security teams in architectural decisions not just in audits. And most importantly, they see cloud security not as a standalone unit, but as an embedded part of product and infrastructure strategy.

When I first started working on cloud systems, I was surprised at how often security decisions were postponed or neglected entirely. Engineers would focus on performance, scalability, and uptime; critical metrics, no doubt but would treat security as something to figure out later. The result was predictable: rushed patches, technical debt, and sometimes catastrophic data exposures. These were not incompetent teams. They were smart, fast-moving, and well-intentioned. But they were operating without a security-first foundation.

At the core of secure cloud development are a few timeless principles, confidentiality, integrity, and availability, often referred to as the CIA triad. These concepts are not new. But in cloud environments, they take on new dimensions. Ensuring confidentiality, for instance, is not just about encryption. It's about who has access, how access is granted, and whether that access is monitored in real-time. Integrity is no longer limited to data validation, it extends to how infrastructure is managed as code, how secrets are stored, and how deployment pipelines are protected. Availability, meanwhile, goes beyond uptime. It includes how systems respond to attacks, how redundancies are built, and how recoveries are orchestrated when things go wrong.

These principles must be embedded at every layer; from application code to infrastructure configuration, from user access policies to automated security scans. And just as important, they must be understood by every team contributing to the system. Security is no longer the job of one team; it is the responsibility of everyone involved in building digital systems.

1.1 Rethinking Security Ownership and Cloud Culture

I remember working with a mid-sized fintech company that had just completed a major cloud migration. Their excitement was palpable. They had scaled their infrastructure, cut costs on physical servers, and reduced deployment times by more than 60 percent. But when we began the post-migration audit, it quickly became clear that while they had moved to the cloud, they had not yet embraced the cloud mindset. Admin credentials were being passed in plaintext through scripts. Access tokens were stored in shared spreadsheets. Network security groups were left wide open "just for testing" and then forgotten.

This isn't a unique story. In fact, it's one I've seen play out time and again across industries. The technical tools are evolving, but many teams are still operating with habits formed in a different era where security lived in silos and developers didn't need to think about IAM policies or encryption standards. In the cloud, that distance is dangerous. The architecture is more dynamic. The attack surface is broader. And mistakes are far easier to scale.

That's why the foundation of secure cloud development begins not with a tool, but with a shift in thinking. It requires acknowledging that every decision, every permission, every deployment, every API exposed is a security decision. It means bringing security into the earliest planning conversations, not waiting until a pen test fails or a compliance deadline loom. It requires asking harder questions up front: Who will need access to this system? How will data be protected in transit and at rest? What happens if this service goes down or worse, if it's breached?

This shift also means rethinking how we define ownership. In the old model, the security team "owned" protection, while everyone else focused on performance and delivery. But in modern cloud-native environments, everyone owns security. Developers own it in their code. DevOps teams own it in their infrastructure automation. Product managers own it in their feature decisions. Executives own it in their investment priorities. When ownership is distributed, accountability becomes cultural. And culture is what sustains a security-first mindset long after audits and compliance checks have passed.

Of course, mindset alone isn't enough. It must be supported by structure and cloud architecture gives us that opportunity. Unlike traditional systems, cloud platforms are built for abstraction, orchestration, and scale. That can be risky if poorly managed, but it can also be a gift. Through Infrastructure as Code (IaC), teams can define secure environments as templates, rather than as one-off builds. Through version control, they can track every configuration change. Through automation, they can enforce security policies without relying on manual intervention.

This is why I've always believed that cloud security, done well, is not just a protection mechanism, it's a competitive advantage. It allows teams to innovate confidently, knowing they are not building brittle foundations. It allows businesses to respond to threats faster, recover from incidents quicker, and meet regulatory requirements with less friction. Most importantly, it sends a message to users and stakeholders alike: we take your trust seriously.

Trust, after all, is the currency of the digital age. And nothing erodes that trust faster than a breach.

Still, building secure systems doesn't mean eliminating risk. That's impossible. What it means is managing risk intentionally. It means understanding the trade-offs between usability and control, between access and oversight, between speed and scrutiny and making those trade-offs deliberately, not by default.

In one particular project, I worked with a health-tech startup building a cloud-native diagnostic platform. They were handling highly sensitive patient data, and regulations were strict. But their team was small, and their timelines were aggressive. They were worried that introducing too many security checks would slow them down. So, we worked together to find balance. We built out secure IAM roles using the least privilege principles. We automated data encryption at rest and in transit. We integrated security checks into their CI/CD pipeline, so developers could catch misconfigurations early without leaving their workflow. We didn't aim for perfection. We aimed for resilience. And it worked. They deployed on time, passed their compliance audit, and never experienced a major security incident.

That project taught me something important: secure development is not about locking things down. It's about enabling progress safely.

One of the most overlooked aspects of cloud architecture is how quickly its environment changes even without direct human involvement. In traditional setups, deployments were infrequent, infrastructure was fixed, and access paths were limited and known. There was time to prepare, time to review, and time to react. But cloud systems don't wait. They scale up and down automatically. Resources are provisioned and destroyed in seconds. Temporary computing environments serve short-term needs and vanish. APIs expand, integrate, and evolve sometimes without full visibility. What you had at 9 AM might look completely different by 4 PM.

This dynamism is part of what makes cloud so powerful but it's also what makes it risky. It expands the threat surface in ways that are difficult to predict. If an organization is still approaching this environment with yesterday's security model static firewalls, hard-coded IP lists, and soiled authentication they're inviting failure. The perimeter has disappeared. In its place is a constantly shifting mesh of services, users, identities, and connections.

Zero Trust starts with a bold but necessary assumption: no one and nothing is automatically trusted, no matter where the request originates. Whether a user is sitting inside the corporate VPN or an internal service is making a request to another internal service, every identity must be authenticated, every action authorized, and every transaction logged. Trust becomes granular. Conditional. Temporary. And above all, earned.

I had a firsthand encounter with the consequences of implicit trust while consulting for a financial intelligence platform that had recently expanded to multiple regions. The system handled vast amounts of real-time transaction data, some of which was regulated by cross-border data laws. On paper, their cloud infrastructure was elegant fast, scalable, and modular. But underneath, it was stitched together with broad IAM permissions, long-lived service accounts, and minimal segmentation. One misstep, a rogue internal script with too many privileges led to unauthorized data exposure across two regions. No breach. But a warning shot.

That incident catalyzed a full re-architecture. We introduced the least privilege access across all services. We moved to federated identity and time-limited tokens for all sensitive operations. Audit logging was centralized and monitored. Every internal service had to verify its permissions through a policy engine before accessing data regardless of how "safe" its environment appeared. It took time. It took investment. It broke some assumptions. But it ultimately created a safer, more transparent system.

Zero Trust isn't about paranoia. It's about preparation. In cloud development, that preparation starts with redefining the concept of boundaries. You no longer defend the gates, you defend every door, every corridor, every interaction.

Equally important is understanding the **shared responsibility model** of cloud platforms. One of the most common misunderstandings I encounter, especially in mid-sized businesses, is the assumption that the cloud provider handles all aspects of security. It doesn't. While providers like AWS, Microsoft Azure, and Google Cloud secure the infrastructure *they* control (hardware, global networks, core services), the customer is still responsible for the configuration, protection, and monitoring of everything built on top of it. That includes data, applications, identities, and access policies.

So, when an S3 bucket is misconfigured and publicly exposed, that's not Amazon's mistake. When a developer hardcodes secrets into a Git repository, that's not Google's fault. The provider gives you the tools but the implementation, oversight, and accountability rest with you.

The sooner organizations internalize this; the sooner they can begin to build cloud systems with proper defenses in place. Because in the end, it's not just about keeping attackers out, it's about building systems that don't collapse when something goes wrong.

And something *will* go wrong.

That's not pessimism, it's reality. Security is not a promise of invincibility. It is a posture of resilience.

1.2 Embedding Security into Architecture and Team Habits

If the cloud demands anything, it is discipline.

Unlike legacy environments where infrastructure was slow to change and change was easier to track; cloud systems thrive on fluidity. They evolve, scale, and connect across multiple services and stakeholders at once. This makes security configuration no longer a set-and-forget activity, but a continuous process embedded into how teams build, test, and deploy their work. The difference between a secure system and a vulnerable one often lies in how early and how consistently security practices are introduced into the workflow.

One of the most misunderstood truths about cloud development is that security doesn't have to be expensive, it has to be intentional.

During a project with a Nigerian health analytics firm, I noticed that the development team was doing an excellent job of writing modular, reusable code. But their security approach was fragmented. Credentials were stored in different places. There were no consistent guidelines for setting IAM roles. Each team had its own version of "best practices," and there was no automated process to check for misconfigurations before deploying updates. Despite their best intentions, the system had grown into something fragile.

What helped was not just deploying tools but introducing patterns.

We implemented secrets management through a centralized system with role-based access controls. We used environment-specific policies to prevent test credentials from ever making it into production. Most importantly, we built security scanning into their development pipeline. These weren't dramatic changes. In fact, they cost less than a single penetration test. But over time, they created consistency. Security became less about fear and more about hygiene, just another part of how good code got written.

These moments taught me something I've carried into every project since: architecture is important, but habits are everything.

You can have the best security blueprint in the world, but if developers bypass controls to "move faster," or if no one reviews logs, or if the same admin password is reused across environments, the blueprint doesn't matter. Culture beats configuration.

That's why secure cloud development has to include a human component. It's not just about systems, it's about practices. Do teams know how to escalate when they see something suspicious? Are policies documented in ways that engineers can actually follow? Is there time budgeted for security reviews during sprint planning? Is security part of the onboarding process?

In other words: is security part of the language of the organization, or is it just background noise?

The companies that do this well are rarely the ones with the most tools, they're the ones where engineers feel confident talking about security without fear of blame or ridicule. Where the security team doesn't just say "no," but explains the "why." Where business goals include risk posture metrics, not just revenue and velocity.

The cloud gives us flexibility. But flexibility without boundaries creates chaos. Security gives shape to that flexibility. And when applied early and consistently, it does more than protect systems it builds maturity.

Every organization wants to move faster. That's the promise of the cloud reduced friction, increased velocity, instant scalability. But what often goes unspoken is this: speed without discipline leads to fragility. And in security, fragility is costly.

Cloud-native systems are not inherently insecure. In fact, they offer more tools, more control, and more transparency than ever before. But these advantages only materialize when they're used intentionally, when teams invest in the culture, the processes, and the architecture that make security part of how software is conceived, not just how it's audited.

I've met brilliant developers who could write flawless infrastructure scripts but didn't know how to spot privilege escalation paths. I've seen security teams overloaded with tickets from preventable misconfigurations. I've seen business leaders approve cloud migrations based purely on cost savings, only to face penalties from regulators a year later. These aren't failures of intelligence, they're failures of alignment. Everyone is running, but not always in the same direction.

To build for the cloud is to accept that change is constant. But to secure the cloud is to ensure that change doesn't come at the cost of safety. That means rethinking incentives, redefining roles, and above all, reestablishing what "done" looks like. A deployment isn't done when the app works. It's done when the data is safe, the access is logged, and the risks are known and managed.

Organizations that internalize this build what I call **security maturity** not in the sense of bureaucracy or compliance, but in the sense of confidence. Mature teams can respond faster to threats. They recover quicker from incidents. They adapt without losing control. And they collaborate across functions with mutual respect.

That maturity doesn't happen overnight. It begins with small choices: checking configurations before pushing code. Using short-lived credentials. Documenting architecture decisions. Asking hard questions. Making time for training. Reviewing not just what went wrong but what almost went wrong and didn't.

This book is not a step-by-step checklist for perfect security. That doesn't exist. What it offers instead is a way of thinking a way of integrating security into your cloud development lifecycle without sacrificing creativity, innovation, or speed.

We've only just begun.

Chapter Two

The Anatomy of Cloud Infrastructure

Most conversations about cloud computing begin with abstraction. The cloud is designed to hide its complexity providing developers and users with clean interfaces, managed services, and seemingly endless scalability. But beneath that simplicity lies one of the most intricate digital ecosystems ever created.

And if you're going to secure it, you have to understand how it's built.

One of the biggest mistakes teams make when moving to the cloud is treating it as a monolith, something singular, uniform, and self-contained. In reality, cloud infrastructure is layered. It includes multiple moving parts each with its own configuration, dependencies, and security requirements. And as you climb the stack from physical infrastructure to software services, the responsibility shifts from the provider to the customer.

At the lowest layer, you have **Infrastructure as a Service (IaaS)**. This is where virtual machines, block storage, and basic networking live. Here, users are responsible for everything from OS-level patches to firewall rules. It resembles traditional server management but with automation and scale baked in. IaaS offers flexibility but also comes with the most security responsibility.

Above that, you have **Platform as a Service (PaaS)**. This layer abstracts away the operating system, letting developers focus on code while the provider manages runtime environments, patches, and some elements of scaling. It's cleaner, faster, and in some ways safer but only if the configurations are done correctly.

And at the top sits **Software as a Service (SaaS)**tools like email systems, document sharing platforms, CRM suites. These are highly abstract, meaning users often have very limited control over backend systems but they still bear responsibility for access controls, data integrity, and user behavior.

Each of these models (IaaS, PaaS, SaaS) comes with its own trade-offs. More control means more responsibility. More abstraction means easier management, but also less visibility into potential risks. A misconfigured PaaS deployment can expose just as much data as an unpatched IaaS server.

And then there are the newer layers **containers**, **serverless functions**, **orchestration tools** like Kubernetes. These technologies have revolutionized how modern applications are deployed. They're faster, lighter, and more portable. But they also introduce new types of vulnerabilities such as overly permissive container configurations, insecure images, or broken isolation between services.

The flexibility of cloud infrastructure is both its strength and its danger. Teams can spin up an entire production environment in minutes. But with every service added, every port opened, every IAM role created, complexity grows. And complexity when left unchecked is the birthplace of security debt.

In my early work with a fintech startup, I joined a team that had adopted Kubernetes before fully understanding it. On the surface, everything worked. Containers deployed correctly. Services were accessible. But behind the scenes, their kubelet API was exposed to the internet, and admin access was left unprotected. It was only during a routine penetration test that the vulnerability surfaced. A single exposed endpoint could have compromised the entire cluster. It wasn't a code issue. It was an architectural blind spot.

That's why cloud architecture is not just about what you build but how you build it, and whether you actually understand the terrain you're operating on.

2.1 Core Components

To truly grasp cloud security, you need to understand the anatomy of what you're protecting. While every cloud provider has its own naming conventions and feature sets, the foundational components are generally the same: **compute**, **networking**, and **storage**. Each is a building block. Each can be a fortress or a flaw.

At its core, the computer refers to the virtual machines, containers, and serverless functions that run workloads. In Infrastructure as a Service (IaaS), this typically means EC2 instances on AWS, Virtual Machines on Azure, or Compute Engine on Google Cloud. In Platform as a Service (PaaS), you might be using App Services or Cloud Run.

The security risks here often stem from **mismanaged images**, **unpatched operating systems**, or **open remote access ports**. I've seen teams deploy powerful instances but forget to disable SSH accessor worse, expose the admin port to the entire internet. These are avoidable errors, but they happen frequently often because compute resources are spun up quickly, tested, then left running in a "temporary" state that becomes permanent.

Containers, meanwhile, offer efficiency but come with their own set of risks. Insecure base images, unscanned dependencies, or containers running as root can all introduce vulnerabilities. When containers are orchestrated at scale, especially with Kubernetes, those risks multiply if proper role-based access control (RBAC) or namespace isolation isn't enforced.

Networking is the circulatory system of the cloud. It controls how services talk to each other, how users access applications, and how traffic flows through your architecture. When configured well, it creates secure pathways and controlled exposure. When done poorly, it becomes an open invitation to attackers.

In cloud environments, virtual networks (VNets in Azure, VPCs in AWS) simulate on-premise segmentation. But unlike traditional networks, they're software-defined and infinitely customizable. This flexibility is powerful but also fragile. The most common misconfiguration I've seen. Overly permissive security groups and firewalls. Developers will often open entire IP ranges or leave default ports accessible for testing then forget to remove them.

DNS misconfigurations are another issue. Improperly secured domains or exposed metadata services can lead to privilege escalation attacks. Even basic routing decisions like failing to use private subnets or route sensitive traffic through internal gateways can weaken security posture significantly.

And in the age of distributed teams and hybrid workloads, managing VPNs, peering connections, and public/private endpoint exposure becomes even more critical. One exposed API gateway, left unprotected, can unravel the entire structure.

While computing powers your applications, and networking connects them, storage is where your most valuable asset resides **data**.

In cloud infrastructure, storage usually takes the form of object storage (like AWS S3, Azure Blob, or GCP Cloud Storage), block storage (volumes attached to compute), and database storage (managed or self-hosted). Object storage is where most headlines have been made and for good reason.

Misconfigured storage buckets have led to some of the biggest data breaches in the past decade. Publicly exposed files, sensitive environment variables stored in plaintext, unencrypted backups all common. All preventable.

What makes this worse is that storage is often **invisible** once it's set. Unlike compute, which developers interact with constantly, storage configurations tend to be created once and forgotten. But attackers know where to look. They use automated tools to scan for exposed buckets, open permissions, or files that contain credentials. And they usually find them.

If the cloud's core components compute, network, and storage form the bones of cloud infrastructure, then orchestration, identity, and automation are the nervous system. They determine how fast you can move, how safely you can scale, and how much risk you carry when things go wrong. They are the levers of control, but also the vectors of error when misunderstood.

Modern applications don't run on a single server, they run across clusters, containers, and regions. Orchestration tools like **Kubernetes**, **AWS ECS**, **Azure AKS**, or **Docker Swarm** make this possible. They automate deployment, scaling, load balancing, and lifecycle management for containers and services.

But orchestration also introduces abstraction and with it, blind spots.

During an audit for a global logistics platform, I came across a Kubernetes cluster with no RBAC controls in place. Any developer with access to the cluster could view, edit, and delete configurations across all namespaces. What began as a cost-saving DevOps project had evolved into a sprawling, uncontrolled mesh of microservices. The team didn't realize they had created a single point of failure until an outage took down their payment gateway and no one could trace the root cause because logging hadn't been configured properly.

Orchestration isn't dangerous by default, but it *amplifies* the impact of every mistake. A misconfigured pod template might go unnoticed in testing, but when deployed to dozens of nodes across multiple regions, it can expose sensitive data or break production traffic at scale. That's why securing orchestration layers means treating configuration as code and policy enforcement as critical infrastructure.

If there's one component that attackers consistently exploit, it's identity.

Cloud environments rely heavily on Identity and Access Management (IAM) systems. These define who (or what) can access which resources and under what conditions. Done well, IAM enforces least privilege, separation of duties, and auditability. Done poorly, it becomes the biggest vulnerability in your stack.

Misused IAM roles, overly permissive policies, long-lived access tokens, or credential leakage in source control are common and dangerous. One of the most sobering lessons I learned early in my career was during a red team simulation for a banking client. The attacker didn't use any zero-day exploit. They gained access through a leaked token with excessive permissions originally issued for a long-forgotten test script.

The breach scenario was simulated, but the point was real: if identity is compromised, your perimeter is irrelevant.

Cloud platforms now support granular IAM features attribute-based access control, service identities, session policies, and more. But these tools are only as strong as the policies behind them. Many organizations default to "admin" or wildcard privileges because it's faster. And in doing so, they create risk profiles that no firewall can fix.

IAM should be viewed not as a formality, but as a gatekeeper. Every role assigned, every key issued, and every permission granted should be tracked, time-bound, and justified.

One of the most powerful benefits of the cloud is automation. You can provision infrastructure with a single command. You can trigger builds, run security scans, roll out updates all without human intervention. Tools like Terraform, Ansible, CloudFormation, and CI/CD pipelines make modern operations fluid.

But automation also removes friction and friction, when properly placed, prevents disaster.

Automation becomes dangerous when it's treated as a shortcut instead of a system. For instance, I once worked with a tech team that automated database provisioning. It saved time but they forgot to include encryption settings in their templates. For weeks, new production databases were being created without any encryption at rest. No one noticed because automation, while efficient, doesn't ask questions.

This is why Infrastructure as Code (IaC) should never be used without policy as code. Tools like Open Policy Agent (OPA) or Sentinel allow you to set guardrails enforcing tagging, encryption, resource boundaries, and compliance checks automatically during provisioning. Automation should speed you up, but it should never make it easier to make irreversible mistakes.

2.2 Observability, Visibility, and the End of Obscurity

In the world of cloud infrastructure, what you can't see can and eventually will hurt you.

The scale and abstraction that make cloud computing powerful also make it easy to lose sight of what's happening beneath the surface. Unlike traditional infrastructure, where sysadmins could physically trace problems through machines and cables, cloud systems stretch across APIs, containers, microservices, and ephemeral resources. Logs, metrics, and events replace manual inspection. Monitoring replaces physical access. And observability becomes the foundation of everything.

But observability is not just about collecting data. It's about making sense of it. It's about connecting what's happening to why it's happening and being able to act on it before small anomalies become systemic failures.

I once conducted a post-incident review with a startup that had suffered a multi-hour outage. Their logs were technically being generated. Metrics were being collected. But the systems weren't integrated. No one was watching them in real time. And the dashboard that might have flagged the issue was hidden in a private workspace no one accessed. By the time the team noticed the problem, customer data was at risk and service-level agreements had been breached.

In that moment, it became clear: **visibility without access is blindness in disguise**.

To build secure cloud infrastructure, you need observability baked in from the start. This includes centralized logging, real-time monitoring, alerting, and a clear policy on who sees what and when. It also means thinking beyond uptime tracking authentication failures, policy changes, privilege escalations, and other behaviors that might signal an emerging threat.

But visibility isn't just for the security team. Developers, DevOps engineers, and architects all need windows into the systems they build. Security improves when everyone can see what's happening and respond accordingly.

That's why "security through obscurity" is one of the most dangerous myths in cloud environments.

Obscurity might feel safe. You hide configurations. You limit access. You bury service endpoints deep in your environment. But obscurity is not protection. It's just a delay.

Attackers today don't need a tour of your systems. They scan. They crawl. They test permissions on a scale. If a port is open or an endpoint is exposed, they will find it whether or not you documented it internally. And when something goes wrong, obscurity makes recovery harder. Teams don't know where things are. Dependencies are undocumented. Logs are inaccessible. And that lack of clarity multiplies downtime and damage.

The better strategy is **deliberate transparency with structured control**. Know what services exist. Know who has access. Document your dependencies. Expose what must be exposed but protect it with policies, alerts, and authentication. Trust visibility, not vagueness.

The most secure teams I've worked with don't hide their systems from each other. They build dashboards that show key activity across environments. They give developers access to error logs without compromising secrets. They track system health alongside system risk. And because they see more, they react faster.

Cloud security isn't just about building better defenses. It's about building better awareness.

The cloud gives us power, but it demands understanding. Not just an abstract understanding of how services work in theory but a concrete, day-to-day awareness of how our systems are structured, how they're connected, and how they're exposed. This isn't about memorizing every service name or mastering every provider's dashboard. It's about owning your architecture end to end.

I've worked with teams that had excellent intentions but incomplete visibility. They deployed services they didn't fully control. They left defaults unchanged. They assumed that "managed" meant "secured." And they built systems that functioned until the day they didn't.

What always struck me in those moments wasn't the severity of the technical flaw, but how often it came down to simple architectural oversight. A misconfigured role. An unmonitored port. A dependency that went undocumented. Each by itself seemed minor. But together, they formed cracks. And as the system grew, so did the risks hide in those cracks.

That's why this chapter, while deeply technical in content, is ultimately about mindset. You cannot secure what you do not understand. And you cannot understand what you do not own.

Whether your team is deploying a simple web application or architecting a distributed multi-cloud platform, the principle is the same: map your infrastructure, document your flows, monitor your changes, and build with clarity. Cloud security isn't just a feature it's the reflection of every architectural decision you've made up to that point.

So, ask yourself:

- Do we know what's running right now?
- Do we know who has access to it?
- Do we know what would happen if something failed?
- And do we have the visibility to act when it does?

Because every cloud breach I've ever studied started with the same problem: something got overlooked.

Chapter Three

Threat Landscape in the Cloud Era

Not too long ago, cloud systems were considered niche too new, too unproven, and too peripheral for serious attackers to focus on. Legacy systems, enterprise data centers, and on-premise servers were the primary battlegrounds for threat actors. Breaches were often the result of malware-laced emails, brute-force attacks on exposed ports, or outdated software that hadn't seen a patch in years.

But that era is over.

The cloud is no longer on the sidelines of digital infrastructure it is the main stage. And with that rise to prominence, it has become a prime target.

Today's attackers are not guessing. They know exactly where to look and what to exploit. They understand the tools engineers use, the mistakes developers often make, and the speed at which cloud environments change. Their goal is not just to break systems, it's to find missteps and move faster than the response.

This is the uncomfortable truth many organizations face: their greatest security risks are no longer complex zero-day vulnerabilities, but simple, avoidable oversights made in high-speed, high-pressure development cycles.

I've seen production keys accidentally pushed to public GitHub repositories. I've seen admin dashboards left exposed with no password protection because someone disabled authentication for testing and forgot to turn it back on. I've seen default credentials reused across dozens of services. And I've seen logs filled with warning signs that no one was watching.

In each of these cases, the cloud didn't create the vulnerability. But it **amplified** it.

The very qualities that make cloud computing attractive its speed, flexibility, automation, and scalability also make it more vulnerable when something is misconfigured. And attackers have adapted to this reality with ruthless efficiency. They use bots to scan open S3 buckets, public Docker containers, unsecured APIs, and misconfigured access controls. They exploit the lag between deployment and security review. They capitalize on overworked teams, poor visibility, and a false sense of "default" safety.

One of the most striking breach stories I studied involved a growing fintech startup. Their engineers had moved quickly, perhaps too quickly, spinning up a containerized infrastructure on a managed cloud service. In the rush to meet a deadline, they bypassed some security protocols and left several containers running in privileged mode. When a single third-party script in their CI/CD pipeline was compromised, the attacker used those permissions to escalate access and pivot across the environment eventually reaching customer data stored in what the team thought was a "low risk" staging database.

The breach didn't come from a high-end exploit. It came from haste.

This is the landscape we now operate in a landscape where security is no longer about just guarding the gates but understanding the full lifecycle of how services are built, deployed, connected, and monitored. The attack surface is not one thing. It is everything. From your IAM policies to your error logs, your third-party integrations to your backups everything is in scope.

And that means we need to think differently.

3.1 Misconfigurations and Credential Exposure

When people think of cybersecurity threats, they often picture sophisticated hacking tools, advanced malware, or dark web attackers deploying zero-day exploits. But in the cloud, the biggest threat isn't complexity it's carelessness. And nowhere is this more evident than in the rising tide of **cloud misconfigurations** and **credential exposure incidents**.

A misconfiguration is not a malicious act. It's usually a rushed decision, a forgotten setting, or a misunderstood permission. But in the cloud, a single misconfiguration can become a breach vector overnight.

In cloud environments, where services are provisioned quickly and teams move fast, the risk of misconfiguration rises dramatically. A study by IBM found that nearly **95% of cloud security breaches were traced back to human error** and the vast majority of those were related to misconfigurations.

Why is this so common?

Because the cloud is **easy to use but hard to master**. Most platforms provide generous defaults for accessibility, assuming the user will harden things later. But "later" rarely comes. And as environments grow more complex with more services, more endpoints, more access roles the chances of a misstep increase.

What makes misconfigurations dangerous is their **invisibility**. Unlike malware, they don't announce themselves. They sit quietly until an attacker finds them first.

If misconfiguration is leaving the door open, **credential leaks** are handing attackers the keys. And unfortunately, it happens far more often than most teams are willing to admit.

One of the most common vectors is credential exposure through source code. Developers, in a rush to test a new integration or feature, will hardcode API tokens, cloud secrets, or database passwords directly into their scripts. These scripts get committed to version control. And in some cases, they get pushed to public repositories.

I once worked with a startup that had accidentally published their entire .env file containing AWS access keys, database credentials, and Stripe API tokens to GitHub. The file was removed within hours, but not before an attacker found it using a bot that scans new commits for secrets. Within a day, fake transactions were being processed, and the team had to rotate all credentials and notify their users.

And it's not just code repos. Credentials leak through chat apps, screenshots, email chains, logs, and misconfigured monitoring dashboards. Long-lived tokens, shared service accounts, and reused passwords only worsen the problem.

Credential theft doesn't require force. It requires opportunity. And in fast-moving cloud environments, opportunity often comes gift-wrapped.

The solution isn't just better secrets management though that's a start. It's **changing the team culture** around how credentials are issued, stored, rotated, and revoked. Teams must move toward **short-lived tokens**, **role-based access**, and **automated secret scanning tools** that catch leaks before they go public.

The more complex a cloud system becomes, the more it relies on connections. Services talk to services. External applications integrate with internal APIs. Systems ingest, transform, and pass data between environments in real time. And while this interconnectedness drives innovation and speed, it also introduces a growing class of security vulnerabilities starting with **insecure APIs**.

APIs are the glue of modern cloud architecture. They enable everything from mobile apps to third-party integrations, from automation scripts to user-facing dashboards. But they're also one of the most exposed components of any cloud system and often one of the least secured.

I've encountered production APIs with no rate limiting, no authentication, and full access to sensitive records. In one case, a financial reporting API allowed users to submit a GET request with a modified account ID parameter and pull any customer's transaction history. There were no checks, no role validation, no scope restriction. Just blind trust in the user's input.

These vulnerabilities aren't uncommon. In fact, **API attacks are one of the fastest-growing vectors in cloud breaches**, according to both OWASP and industry threat reports. What makes them especially dangerous is their legitimacy. Attackers don't need to "break in, they use the front door. They send valid requests to valid endpoints and exploit what the system allows.

Cloud platforms often expose dozens sometimes hundreds of APIs. Many are forgotten, undocumented, or assumed to be "internal only." But in cloud environments, "internal" is a moving target. A misconfigured route, a public gateway, or a leaked token can turn an internal API into a public vulnerability in seconds.

Defending against API threats requires **visibility, testing, and strict control**. Teams need to know what endpoints exist, what permissions they accept, and how they handle invalid or malicious input. This isn't just a backend concern, it's a security posture decision.

We often think of cyberattacks as external, a nameless attacker trying to breach the system from the outside. But in many cloud security incidents, the real danger comes from within.

Insider threats are difficult to detect because they often involve legitimate access used for illegitimate purposes. A former employee retains access to admin panels after offboarding. A DevOps engineer uses elevated permissions to explore data outside their scope. A trusted contractor stores copies of configuration files locally. These actions might not even be malicious, they may be careless, rushed, or unintentional. But the outcome is the same: a breach of trust, control, and data.

In cloud systems, where access is role-based, automated, and often broad by default, **insider risks increase** when access controls aren't clearly defined or aggressively maintained. I once audited a company where nearly half of the engineering team had full admin rights across production systems. No logging. No role separation. No restrictions.

If even one person in that group had made a mistake or acted maliciously the entire infrastructure was vulnerable.

Preventing insider threats isn't about paranoia. It's about **least privilege**, clear **audit trails**, and consistent **offboarding protocols**. People need access to do their jobs, but they don't need more than that. And when they leave, access should go with them.

The final threat in this trio is subtler but just as dangerous: **lack of visibility**.

As cloud systems scale, they often fragment. Teams deploy in silos. Services span regions and accounts. Monitoring tools cover part of the infrastructure, but not all. Logs are written, but no one reads them. Alerts are generated, but no one owns the response. Over time, **blind spots form** and attackers thrive in those blind spots.

I've walked into post-breach reviews where the biggest revelation wasn't how the attacker got in it was how long they had gone undetected. In one case, it was **42 days** before anyone noticed abnormal activity and by then, credentials had been harvested, logs had been wiped, and the damage was done.

Visibility isn't a luxury. It's the only way to defend what you've built. That means centralizing logs. Aggregating metrics. Setting thresholds. Automating alerts. And, most importantly, assigning ownership to what those alerts trigger.

Because the best defense in cloud security is knowing what's happening before it makes the headlines.

3.2 Third-Party Integrations and Supply Chain Attacks

Cloud systems don't operate in isolation. They integrate, connect, and depend on APIs, SDKs, plugins, libraries, platforms, and external vendors. And while this modularity makes cloud development faster and more scalable, it also introduces one of the most dangerous and difficult threats to detect: the **supply chain attack**.

A supply chain attack happens when a trusted third-party component whether it's a software dependency, an open-source package, or a cloud vendor is compromised and used as a backdoor into your system. The attacker doesn't go after *you*. They go after what you trust.

The infamous SolarWinds attack in 2020 is a textbook example. Threat actors compromised an update to a widely used IT monitoring platform. That single breach allowed them to silently enter networks across multiple government agencies and Fortune 500 companies. Not because those organizations were insecure but because their supplier was.

In the cloud, these risks multiply. Modern applications rely on dozens of third-party services from authentication platforms to payment gateways, from CDN providers to logging frameworks. And while each one claims security, the truth is: **every new dependency expands your threat surface**.

I've seen cloud environments where CI/CD pipelines were configured to pull builds from external registries with no validation. I've seen authentication flows that depended on deprecated APIs from third-party vendors. In one case, a popular npm package used in a serverless function was hijacked, and malicious code was injected into every deployment downstream.

The risk is real. And the worst part? These threats often **bypass traditional defenses**. They come through trusted channels. They don't trigger firewall alerts. They're invisible until it's too late.

One of the most dangerous assumptions teams make is that if something is widely used, it must be safe. That logic has led to compromised JavaScript libraries being served across thousands of websites, vulnerable container images being reused without checks, and deprecated SDKs persisting in production environments for years.

Cloud development rewards reuse. It encourages "don't reinvent the wheel." But when that wheel is compromised, the fallout is exponential.

This is where **dependency hygiene** becomes critical. Teams must know what they use. They must track package versions. They must audit external services for their own risk exposure. This includes open-source code, SaaS vendors, cloud-based integrations, and even browser extensions used in development environments.

A strong security posture today requires scanning not only what you build but what you borrow.

Mitigation Is Possible But It Requires Discipline

To reduce exposure to supply chain attacks, cloud teams should:

- Maintain a **software bill of materials (SBOM)**a full inventory of dependencies.
- Pin versions and avoid automatic upgrades without review.
- Use trusted registries and verify image signatures for containerized applications.
- Monitor third-party vendors for breach disclosures, service changes, and incident reports.

- Implement dependency scanning tools into the build process and treat flagged issues as production risks, not development nuisances.

The truth is that most cloud compromises today don't happen through brute force. They happen because someone, somewhere, reused a trusted resource that wasn't as secure as it seemed.

The threats we've explored in this chapter misconfigurations, leaked credentials, insider abuse, insecure APIs, and supply chain compromise may seem like different problems on the surface. But underneath, they all stem from the same underlying challenge: cloud systems have outgrown the old ways we used to secure them.

In legacy environments, security was layered on after the fact. You built your system, then added firewalls. You deployed your app, then performed penetration tests. You ran your services, then worried about monitoring. This lag worked when change was slow. It does not work in the cloud.

Today, change is continuous. Cloud systems are updated daily, deployed hourly, and scaled by the minute. Teams are decentralized. The infrastructure is dynamic. And the window for catching vulnerabilities manually is closing fast.

What this means is simple but urgent: security must be a workflow, not a reaction. It must be embedded into how services are designed, coded, deployed, and monitored not left as an afterthought or a bottleneck. This is not a cultural luxury; it is a survival strategy.

Every time a developer spins up a resource, security should be part of that decision. Every time a service is exposed, its access should be intentional. Every time a key is generated, its lifecycle should be limited and logged. Every component should have ownership. Every alert should have a response plan. Every tool should work in concert not just to deliver uptime, but to deliver safety.

And perhaps most importantly: every member of the team should be empowered to ask security questions without fear of slowing things down. Because speed is only valuable when you know where you're going. And in cloud security, the fastest route to disaster is assuming you're already safe.

I've seen what happens when security is built in. Teams move faster, not slower because they don't have to undo costly mistakes. They deploy with confidence. They scale with clarity. They respond to threats with maturity. And they sleep better at night not because nothing will ever go wrong, but because when it does, they're ready.

Chapter Four

Security-by-Design for Cloud Applications

In the fast-paced world of cloud engineering, deadlines are tight, releases are frequent, and the pressure to deliver can overwhelm even the most experienced teams. It's no surprise, then, that security is often treated as something to "bolt on" later, once the code works, once the platform is stable, once the user feedback is positive.

But waiting until "later" is the most expensive security decision you can make.

Security-by-design is the discipline of thinking about protection from the first sketch of an architecture diagram, from the first line of code, from the first conversation about user flows. It's not about adding roadblocks, it's about baking safety into the foundation so that as your application scales, its defenses scale with it.

This mindset isn't new. In fact, it's rooted in old engineering wisdom: build it right the first time. What's changed is the environment. In cloud-native applications, the building blocks are faster, lighter, and more distributed. Services are ephemeral. The infrastructure is programmable. Change is constant. Which means the design phase is no longer a single moment, it's an ongoing, iterative cycle. And in that cycle, security has to be present at every layer.

I've worked with teams that treated security as a final checklist something they handled at the very end of the sprint. Often, it wasn't even the developers who handled it. It was a separate "infosec" team that reviewed the code after deployment and sent a PDF report with remediation steps. By that point, the decisions were already baked in. Changing anything meant delays, and delays meant resistance.

That separation is what security-by-design seeks to eliminate. It brings everyone developers, architects, security professionals into the same process, early and often. It's not about shifting blame. It's about shifting left.

Shifting left is a simple phrase with powerful consequences. It means addressing risks earlier in the development lifecycle, where they are cheaper to fix, easier to understand, and less likely to be ignored. Instead of reacting to vulnerabilities found in production, teams start by asking: how do we prevent this from happening in the first place?

What makes this approach work, especially in the clouds, is proactive. Instead of fighting fires, you prevent them from ever starting.

Security-by-design doesn't eliminate risk. That's not the goal. The goal is to reduce attack surfaces, minimize blast radius, and increase resilience. It's about designing systems with the expectation that something *will* go wrong and ensuring that when it does, the damage is contained, the exposure is minimal, and the recovery is fast.

We'll look at what security-by-design actually looks like in practice from threat modeling and secure defaults to developer enablement and secure architecture patterns. We'll walk through how product decisions impact security posture, and how teams can design systems that don't just meet functional requirements but protect the people who depend on them.

Because in cloud applications, functionality without security is not innovation, it's a liability.

4.1 Threat Modeling: Designing with the Adversary in Mind

Before you build anything secure, you have to imagine how it could break.

That's the essence of threat modeling the practice of thinking like an attacker before you write code, deploy infrastructure, or expose a single API. It's one of the most valuable tools in a cloud architect's toolkit, and yet it's often overlooked because it doesn't "produce" anything. There's no immediate output.

No shipped feature. No visible result. Just a set of conversations, diagrams, and assumptions.

But those assumptions can mean the difference between resilience and exposure.

I first introduced threat modeling to a product team during a redesign of their cloud-based onboarding system. The service worked fine; it verified users, collected data, and triggered internal workflows. But as we began walking through their design diagram, we asked a simple question: *what happens if a user submits malicious input into the onboarding API?* What if the backend failed to validate that input? What if someone intercepted traffic between services? What if the internal workflow service wasn't locked down?

Those questions changed the conversation.

Threat modeling forces you to think in layers. It's not just about what could go wrong but *how*, *where*, *why*, and *what the consequences would be.* In cloud environments where multiple services, functions, and identities interact asynchronously, it's especially important to map out:

- Who the actors are (users, services, admins)
- What assets they're accessing (data, compute resources, configuration)
- What the trust boundaries are (e.g., between front-end and backend, between cloud accounts)

- What could go wrong with each boundary

You don't need to be a security expert to do this. In fact, the best threat modeling sessions I've been part of were led by product managers and developers; people who understood the business logic deeply and just needed the right questions to guide the analysis.

Cloud-native threat modeling should focus on **realistic abuse cases**. Not just theoretical attacks, but patterns that are common in cloud breaches: token theft, overly broad IAM roles, exposed containers, lack of input validation, internal services assuming too much trust.

Tools like **STRIDE**, **PASTA**, or **attack trees** can help structure the process but the real value is in the mindset shift. Instead of asking, *does this work?* teams ask, *what would happen if this failed and who would benefit from that failure?*

When threat modeling becomes a habit, architecture evolves. Teams start placing stronger controls at the points of risk. They isolate services more deliberately. They limit default permissions. They question data flows. They test for misuse, not just malfunction.

I've seen this habit save organizations millions *not* by preventing every threat, but by reducing the number of dangerous assumptions baked into design.

Out of the box, cloud platforms offer incredible speed. You can launch a database in seconds. Spin up a web server with a few clicks. Grant access to an entire project with a single IAM role. These conveniences aren't flaws; their features. But they come with a hidden cost: **default settings that prioritize usability over security**.

In secure system design, one principle matters more than most: **secure by default**.

This means that when no action is taken when the developer forgets, when the admin rushes, when the project is deployed as-is the system should fall into a state of **safety**, not exposure. But that's not how many clouds services work by default. They prioritize onboarding and speed, assuming that the user will harden security afterward. And all too often, they don't.

I once conducted a security review for a media tech company that had deployed multiple storage buckets to AWS S3. They assumed the buckets were private because no one had explicitly shared them. But due to legacy policies, several of those buckets were publicly accessible. Files included raw media assets, user metadata, and temporary session tokens. The company hadn't *chosen* to expose that data, it had simply never changed the default permissions.

This is the problem with insecure defaults: they introduce **passive risk**. A team might not notice. A test environment might go live with open access. An admin might use a wildcard in a policy because it "just works." Every one of these choices is small but together, they accumulate into massive surface area for exploitation.

Designing secure cloud systems means resisting the urge to prioritize speed over structure. It means challenging the defaults provided by your cloud platform, your container image, your CI/CD pipeline tool, your secret management system. And it means having clear policies that define *what the default state should be* especially when no one is looking.

Secure defaults apply to everything:

- Should new storage buckets be encrypted automatically?
- Should public access be disabled by default on new databases?
- Should new IAM users be created without any permissions until explicitly assigned?
- Should audit logging be turned on automatically for new services?

These are not technical questions. They are **design decisions**.

Security-by-design doesn't mean locking everything down unnecessarily. It means building systems where the *easiest* path is also the *safest* one. Where doing the right thing isn't a burden, it's the standard.

When defaults are secure, teams don't need to be perfect. They just need to follow the path of least resistance which, if designed well, leads away from danger.

4.2 Developer Enablement and the Culture of Secure Collaboration

The most secure cloud systems I've seen weren't built by teams with the biggest budgets or the most certifications. They were built by teams where developers felt empowered to care about security and knew how to act on that care.

Security-by-design is not just about technical controls. It's about people, habits, and communication. It's about enabling developers not burdening them with the knowledge, tools, and authority to make secure decisions as part of their daily work.

I've worked with organizations where security was treated like a police department: always watching, rarely collaborating, often arriving late with a list of violations. In that kind of culture, developers don't engage, they avoid. They find workarounds. They fear delays. And eventually, they build without input.

By contrast, teams that excel in security-by-design embed security as a partner in the development lifecycle. They don't isolate the security team, they integrate it. They make security a shared goal, not someone else's problem.

Here's what that looks like in practice:

- Security engineers attend sprint planning sessions, not just incident reviews.
- Developers receive training in secure coding practices early, often, and contextually.
- Linting tools and code scanners run in local environments catching issues before they reach staging.
- CI/CD pipelines flag misconfigurations automatically not just post-deploy.
- Infrastructure templates come with security baked in not added after provisioning.
- IAM decisions are guided by templates and review processes not guesswork or trial and error.

When security knowledge is distributed across the team, you create a **culture of shared accountability**. No one waits until "the security team signs off." Instead, security is *built in* peer-reviewed, automated, and continually improved through feedback loops.

In one cloud-native platform I consulted for, the transformation began with a single decision: the security team created Slack bots that scanned pull requests for known anti-patterns like hardcoded secrets, overly permissive policies, or open API routes. These bots didn't block builds they just dropped a comment in the PR with a suggested fix.

What happened next was powerful: developers started fixing issues *before* the security team even engaged. They learned from the feedback. They challenged it when needed. And within weeks, the volume of critical vulnerabilities in the new code dropped significantly not because anyone worked slower, but because **they worked smarter together**.

Security doesn't scale when it's centralized. It scales when it's **embedded, democratized, and normalized** across every role that touches the system.

That's the real heart of security-by-design: making protection a team sport.

In cloud environments, shipping fast is no longer optional. Businesses demand it. Users expect it. Teams are measured by it. But in the pursuit of velocity, we must remember **speed is only useful if what you're building can survive pressure**.

That's where security-by-design reveals its full value not just as a development strategy, but as a **resilience strategy**.

I've worked with organizations that moved fast but didn't break things. Not because they had perfect developers or unlimited security staff, but because they treated security as an architectural pillar, not a patch job. They modeled threats before launch. They chose safe defaults. They gave their teams the knowledge and tools to build securely without waiting for permission. They weren't immune to mistakes. But when mistakes happened, **the damage was contained**.

That's the difference between reactive security and resilient security.

When you design securely, failures become isolated not systemic. A bad deployment doesn't leak credentials. A compromised API doesn't unlock the database. A rogue user can't reach sensitive data they were never meant to see. And when an incident does occur, the response is faster, clearer, and less chaotic because the groundwork was already laid in the design.

This approach doesn't just protect your systems. It builds **trust** with users, partners, auditors, and even within your team. Developers feel more confident pushing changes. Security teams feel more respected. Business leaders feel less surprised by incidents. And customers feel safer using your product.

And here's the final truth: security-by-design scales.

It doesn't rely on manual inspection of every line of code. It doesn't require perfect humans. It's a pattern a way of thinking that can be encoded into templates, pipelines, policies, and reviews. It becomes easier with time, not harder. And it creates systems that are not just functional, but **durable**.

Chapter Five

Identity Access and Zero Trust in the Cloud

In traditional security models, protection meant building walls; firewalls, data centers, and network zones that kept the "outside" world away from trusted internal systems. That approach worked in a time when infrastructure was static, users were local, and services lived behind fixed IPs.

There is no fixed perimeter. Applications run across regions. Users log in from personal devices. Services are ephemeral and distributed. What defines a system is no longer its physical boundary but who can access what, from where, and under what conditions.

It doesn't matter how strong your encryption is or how tight your firewall rules are if your access controls are weak, everything behind them is vulnerable. That's why modern cloud security begins with identity: **who or what is making the request? What are they allowed to do? And how do we verify that access, every time?**

I've seen organizations with beautifully architected infrastructure redundant, encrypted, scalable. But a single admin token leaked in a Slack message gave an attacker full control. Not because the infrastructure failed. But because **identity was treated as an afterthought**.

And identity in the cloud isn't just about human users. It's about **services**, **functions**, **applications**, and **scripts,** all of which need access to resources, and all of which can be compromised if misconfigured. In most cloud breaches today, the attacker doesn't "break in" through brute force. They **log in** using credentials or tokens that were accidentally exposed, poorly managed, or granted excessive privilege.

This is why the **Zero Trust** model has become essential.

Zero Trust begins with a single radical idea: **no one is trusted by default, not even inside the system**. Every access request must be verified, every identity authenticated, every action authorized. It's a shift from assuming safety to designing for doubt.

When implemented well, Zero Trust does more than reduce risk. It shrinks the blast radius of every breach. If one user is compromised, their access is limited. If one service is hijacked, it can't see or modify unrelated systems. Zero Trust turns a potential disaster into an isolated incident.

5.1 Anatomy of IAM and the Risks of Overprivileged

Identity and Access Management (IAM) serves as the central framework for managing permissions in cloud environments. It governs how users, services, and systems authenticate and what they are authorized to access.

At its core, IAM comprises the following components:

- **Principals**: Entities (such as users, applications, or automated functions) that request access.
- **Resources**: Cloud components such as databases, storage buckets, compute instances, and APIs.
- **Policies**: The rules that define what actions a principal can perform on a resource.
- **Authentication**: The process of verifying identity through credentials, tokens, certificates, or federated systems.
- **Authorization**: The evaluation of policies to determine access rights following successful authentication.

Misconfigurations or oversights in any of these areas can lead to security failures. The most common failure pattern is overprivilege, assigning roles or permissions that are broader than necessary for the task at hand.

This often happens through the use of:

- Wildcard permissions (e.g., s3: * or ec2: *)
- Administrator roles granted by default
- Shared service accounts with no identity isolation
- Long-lived access keys that are never rotated or audited

Such configurations violate the principle of **least privilege**, which states that principals should be granted only the minimum permissions required to perform their function no more, no less.

In fast-paced environments, shortcuts are common. Teams may assign full access to speed up development or use inherited policies without understanding their scope. These shortcuts introduce risk. An attacker who compromises one overprivileged account can potentially access a wide range of systems far beyond what was necessary for that account's legitimate function.

IAM missteps are rarely the result of malicious intent. More often, they stem from a lack of visibility into permission boundaries, poor documentation, or inadequate review processes. In highly dynamic cloud environments, roles and policies evolve rapidly, making it easy for outdated or redundant privileges to persist unnoticed.

In some cases, the problem is not excessive access but unclear ownership. Without proper tagging or grouping, it becomes difficult to determine which services are using which roles, and why those permissions were granted. This lack of transparency undermines auditability and complicates incident response.

Effective IAM design requires discipline, visibility, and continuous enforcement. Role hierarchies must be clearly defined, policies scoped narrowly, and access regularly reviewed for necessity. Automation tools can assist in detecting policy drift or unused privileges, but the underlying architecture must be built with **access intent** in mind.

Excellent. Here's **Part 3/5** of **Chapter Five: Identity, Access, and Zero Trust in the Cloud** from *Cloud-Driven Defense* by Mariam Adetoun Sanusi. This section outlines how **Zero Trust principles** are applied in cloud environments through **segmentation**, **the least privilege**, and **context-aware controls**.

Zero Trust is often misunderstood as a product or a simple framework. In practice, it is a **security philosophy** that guides how systems validate, authorize, and isolate access, especially in cloud-native environments where perimeters are abstract, and users are distributed.

Rather than assuming that a request from within a network is inherently safe, Zero Trust dictates that **every request must be authenticated and authorized regardless of its origin.** Trust is neither implied nor permanent. It must be re-evaluated continually based on identity, context, and risk signals.

The implementation of Zero Trust in the cloud is primarily achieved through three interlocking strategies:

1. Identity-Aware Segmentation

Cloud workloads are highly interconnected, with services often communicating across multiple layers and platforms. Zero Trust introduces segmentation at the **identity** level not just at the network level.

Resources are logically separated by role, environment, or purpose. Access to each segment is governed by fine-grained policies that take into account:

- User or service identity
- Device compliance status
- Time of request
- Geolocation or IP reputation
- Type of resource being requested

This level of segmentation reduces lateral movement. If one service or user is compromised, access to other parts of the system remains limited.

2. Least Privilege and Just-in-Time Access

While the least privilege is a foundational principle of IAM, Zero Trust strengthens it by encouraging **temporal and conditional access**.

Rather than assigning static roles with permanent permissions, access is granted:

- **On demand**, for a specific purpose
- **With scope limitation**, to a defined set of actions or resources
- **With expiration**, after a predefined time period or once a task is complete

Just-in-time access models ensure that no account accumulates excessive privileges over time. They also reduce the risk of dormant credentials being exploited after users change roles or leave the organization.

3. Adaptive and Context-Aware Authorization

In Zero Trust architectures, authorization is not a binary decision. It is **adaptive**, taking into account contextual signals that may indicate unusual or risky behavior.

For example:

- A login request from an unrecognized device may trigger step-up authentication
- A user requesting access to sensitive data outside of business hours may require additional approval
- API calls made at unusually high volume may be temporarily throttled or blocked pending review

These decisions are typically enforced through **policy engines** that evaluate risk signals in real time. Cloud-native platforms offer support for integrating threat intelligence, device posture checks, and geofencing into access decisions.

By combining identity segmentation, time-bound access, and contextual controls, Zero Trust becomes a **dynamic enforcement model** shaping access not only by who a user is, but by what they are doing, when, where, and how.

5.2 Barriers to Implementing Zero Trust Effectively

The advantages of Zero Trust in cloud architecture are well-documented: minimized attack surface, reduced lateral movement, and improved security posture. However, implementation is rarely straightforward. A range of technical, operational, and organizational challenges can delay or dilute adoption.

1. Legacy Systems and Fragmented Environments

Many enterprises operate in hybrid environments that blend modern cloud workloads with on-premise or legacy applications. These legacy systems often lack native support for fine-grained IAM, token-based authentication, or micro segmentation.

In such scenarios, attempts to enforce Zero Trust principles may be constrained by:

- Lack of APIs or connectors for centralized policy enforcement
- Hard-coded access patterns that resist dynamic authorization
- Inconsistent identity schemas across platforms

Workarounds such as identity federation or reverse proxying can help bridge the gap but often introduce complexity and require ongoing maintenance.

2. Tool Sprawl and Policy Inconsistency

Zero Trust is not a single product. It is implemented through a combination of identity providers, access management systems, endpoint detection tools, cloud service policies, and workload segmentation controls.

Without a unified strategy, organizations risk:

- Policy conflicts across platforms (e.g., conflicting IAM rules between AWS and Azure)
- Duplication of role definitions and inconsistent enforcement
- Lack of visibility into who has access to what across environments

This sprawl complicates compliance and makes auditing more difficult. It also increases the likelihood of human error, especially in organizations where security responsibilities are distributed across multiple teams.

3. Organizational Resistance and Change Fatigue

Zero Trust often requires significant shifts in how access is granted, reviewed, and revoked. These changes may be met with friction from teams accustomed to static roles and broad permissions.

Common points of resistance include:

- Concerns about increased friction for developers or analysts
- Perceived delays in getting access to needed resources
- Pushback against frequent re-authentication or additional verification steps

In the absence of clear communication and stakeholder buy-in, Zero Trust initiatives may stall or be undermined by manual exceptions and workarounds.

4. Over-Reliance on Technological Controls

Another common pitfall is assuming that Zero Trust can be fully achieved through tooling alone. Even the most advanced access platforms are ineffective if policies are poorly written, roles are overprovisioned, or review processes are neglected.

Successful Zero Trust implementations are supported by:

- Clear governance models
- Continuous training for developers and administrators
- Defined ownership of access control policies
- Auditing mechanisms that validate policy effectiveness over time

Technology plays a crucial role, but the foundation lies in discipline, accountability, and cultural alignment.

Implementing Zero Trust in cloud environments is not a one-time configuration; it is a continuous, evolving process that must be embedded into the organization's culture and architecture. At the core of this effort is the development of a robust identity and access management strategy, one that aligns with Zero Trust principles while still supporting operational efficiency.

The first step in that strategy is consolidation. Many organizations operate with overlapping identity systems and fragmented access protocols across departments, regions, and services. Consolidating identities into a single, federated system provides a unified source of truth. This not only streamlines authentication workflows but also allows consistent enforcement of access policies across platforms. When users and services are recognized through a common identity provider, it becomes significantly easier to monitor, manage, and audit their behavior.

Policy design must then reflect the principle of least privilege not just in theory, but in practice. This means roles should be tightly scoped and narrowly defined, tailored to specific tasks rather than broad job functions. Access should be granted based on demonstrable need, with all permissions reviewed regularly and removed once they are no longer required. Automation plays a critical role here, especially in large environments where manual access review is prone to oversight and drift. Identity governance tools, when configured correctly, can flag anomalous privilege escalations and trigger timely remediation.

Equally important is the integration of context-aware access decisions. Identity alone is no longer sufficient to determine risk. A complete strategy considers device health, location, time, behavior history, and the sensitivity of the requested resource. For instance, an access request from an unfamiliar device or location might require multi-factor authentication or temporary elevation of scrutiny. Adaptive access not only improves security but also preserves usability, ensuring that the right people have access without unnecessary obstacles while potential threats face increasing resistance.

Training and operational alignment must accompany these technical efforts. Engineers, administrators, and business users alike need to understand the rationale behind access controls and the risks of bypassing them. A Zero Trust model succeeds only when its policies are supported by awareness and accountability. This includes clearly documented escalation procedures, ownership of access decisions, and periodic audits to ensure that controls are doing what they were designed to do.

Finally, resilience must be baked into the architecture. No access strategy is perfect, and breaches may still occur. A mature Zero Trust posture ensures that when compromise happens, its impact is contained. Lateral movement is minimized. Logs are detailed and available. Detection is timely. And recovery is structured.

Cloud systems move fast. Identity, more than any other control surface, defines the boundary of risk. In treating identity as a living, dynamic component of infrastructure subject to the same rigor and iteration as code or data organizations move closer to a defensible cloud posture. Zero Trust, in this light, is not about distrust, it is about discipline. And in today's security landscape, that discipline is the most valuable defense of all.

Chapter Six

Infrastructure as Code and Security Automation

The rise of cloud computing introduced more than just elastic compute resources and scalable storage. It introduced a new paradigm in how infrastructure is conceptualized, managed, and secured. No longer are servers manually provisioned or network rules updated through ticket queues. Instead, infrastructure itself is now programmable declared, versioned, deployed, and destroyed through code.

This approach, known as Infrastructure as Code (IaC), has transformed operations teams into engineering teams and changed the speed at which environments are spun up. But this same power, the ability to deploy entire networks, applications, and permissions in seconds, also carries a heightened responsibility. When infrastructure becomes code, mistakes become repeatable. Misconfigurations become scalable. And security must become automated.

Infrastructure as Code shifts infrastructure from being an operational concern to a **software development practice**. Definitions of resources such as virtual machines, storage buckets, load balancers, and security groups are written in declarative formats like YAML, JSON, or domain-specific languages such as HashiCorp Configuration Language (HCL) for Terraform. These templates can then be versioned, peer-reviewed, tested, and deployed using the same toolchains that govern application code.

The implications for security are profound. First, IaC allows teams to **treat security configurations as artifacts**, not as ad hoc settings. Rather than relying on individuals to manually restrict network ports or configure encryption settings, those specifications are embedded directly in the code. This not only reduces human error but also ensures that security controls are applied consistently across environments.

Second, IaC enables **predictability and repeatability**. A security-hardened environment, once codified, can be deployed reliably to development, staging, and production removing drift between environments. This alignment helps eliminate the common scenario where a vulnerability is fixed in production but left open in test or dev environments due to manual configuration differences.

Third, the code-based nature of IaC supports **auditability and accountability**. Changes to infrastructure pass through version control systems like Git, leaving behind a trail of who modified what, when, and why. Rollbacks are easier, peer reviews become part of security governance, and organizations gain deeper visibility into their infrastructure lifecycle.

However, the shift to IaC is not merely a change in tooling, it is a change in thinking. It demands a mindset where infrastructure is no longer static, no longer managed by memory or habit, but rather **designed with intent**. Security must be embedded at the template level, not bolted on after the fact. And teams must develop the discipline to treat infrastructure artifacts with the same rigor as production code.

6.1 Risks and Realities: When Code Becomes a Security Liability

While Infrastructure as Code offers unmatched speed, transparency, and scalability, it also amplifies risk. When code defines infrastructure, a single misconfiguration can ripple across an entire environment in seconds compromising not just availability but also security. What once would've taken hours to misconfigure by hand can now be deployed into production in moments, automated and persistent.

In practice, many cloud breaches tied to IaC have shared one thing in common: **oversight in the code layer**. Consider a scenario where an engineer mistakenly sets an S3 bucket to "public-read" in a Terraform script. If that template is used across multiple environments, that same insecure setting is now present in staging, QA, and production exposing sensitive customer data to the public internet. Worse still, because the setting was defined in code, it may be viewed as "approved" simply by virtue of being version-controlled.

This is the dual nature of IaC. It promotes consistency but it also propagates flaws. And in cloud systems, where infrastructure is fluid and workloads shift rapidly, small mistakes scale fast.

Security automation seeks to intervene in that scaling process. By embedding checks directly into the development pipeline, organizations can catch misconfigurations **before** code is deployed. Tools like Checkov, tfsec, and AWS Config allow teams to scan IaC templates for violations of best practices flagging open security groups, unrestricted IAM policies, unencrypted storage volumes, and more. These tools act as **policy enforcers**, bringing security into the same workflows where code is built and tested.

However, automation isn't foolproof. Tools can only identify what they're programmed to catch. If a risky configuration isn't explicitly flagged by a policy engine, it may slip through unnoticed. This highlights the need for **human oversight**, especially in reviewing context-specific decisions like whether a database should be externally accessible or if a particular role truly needs admin-level privileges.

There is also the risk of **security fatigue**. If scanning tools produce too many alerts or false positives, engineers may start ignoring the warnings altogether. The solution is not to remove the tools, but to refine them to build policies that are both strict and sensible, tailored to the organization's actual security objectives rather than generic benchmarks.

Another overlooked issue is **template reuse without context reassessment**. A Terraform module created for one project might later be reused in another with vastly different sensitivity requirements. Unless the security assumptions are reevaluated, this reuse introduces silent misalignment. What was once "secure enough" for internal analytics might be dangerously exposed when used for external-facing systems.

To counter this, organizations must treat IaC not as one-off automation, but as **living infrastructure logic** versioned, reviewed, and evolved with awareness of its security posture over time. It requires strong policy libraries, code ownership, change management protocols, and a willingness to challenge the idea that "if it worked last time, it must be safe this time too."

6.2 Bridging Static Code and Dynamic Environments

Writing secure infrastructure code is only half the battle. What gets written in a YAML or HCL file isn't always what ends up running in production. Drift happens either through manual changes made outside of version control, or through services that evolve their state post-deployment. As a result, security assurance requires not just static analysis of code, but also real-time validation of running infrastructure.

To address this, many organizations now adopt a layered approach. The first layer is pre-deployment scanning automated tools that check templates and configurations before they're ever applied. These scans identify hardcoded secrets, overly permissive IAM roles, public-facing assets, and insecure storage configurations. They're fast, cheap to run, and easy to integrate into CI/CD pipelines. But they're limited to what the code says, not what the cloud environment actually looks like after deployment.

That's where dynamic validation comes in. Post-deployment tools like AWS Config, Azure Policy, and custom runtime monitors continuously evaluate cloud resources against compliance baselines. For instance, a virtual machine spun up with encryption disabled may pass the initial template scan, but once live, can be flagged and remediated by policy enforcement agents. This creates a feedback loop allowing organizations to detect deviations, trigger alerts, and in some cases, automatically roll back or quarantine insecure resources.

Still, maintaining alignment between IaC and deployed infrastructure is not just a technical challenge; it's a governance challenge. Without clear ownership and communication, teams may not know whether a resource was deliberately changed outside of code or accidentally misconfigured. That's why modern DevSecOps teams treat cloud security as a continuous state not a checkbox that gets ticked during the deployment stage. They monitor the actual infrastructure posture at all times and compare it to what's defined in code, surfacing any mismatches as risks to be resolved.

Continuous compliance frameworks further support this discipline. In regulated industries like finance, healthcare, government real-time evidence of security controls is required. Cloud-native services now allow for automated compliance tracking: infrastructure states, access logs, encryption status, and network flows can all be captured and reported in near real-time. This makes audits smoother, but more importantly, it reinforces good security hygiene. Teams can't hide behind the assumption that deployment equals protection.

Another vital concept in this domain is policy-as-code. Just as infrastructure is declared as code, so are the rules that govern it. Instead of relying on informal security guidelines, teams can codify policies into the deployment process. If a security group exposes port 22 to the world, a policy written in Rego (for tools like Open Policy Agent) can automatically reject that configuration before it ever reaches the cloud provider. This turns subjective security "best practices" into enforceable gates.

The first step in operationalizing security automation is to embed it directly into the development pipeline. This means integrating IaC scanning tools into continuous integration (CI) systems so that every pull request triggers automated checks for misconfigurations or policy violations. Rather than waiting until deployment to discover a mistake, engineers are notified during code review when the fix is simpler, cheaper, and less disruptive.

But automation must be opinionated to be useful. Generic checks often flood teams with alerts, many of which lack context or urgency. To prevent alert fatigue, teams must define tailored security baselines aligned with their specific risks. For example, an e-commerce platform may place stronger restrictions around payment processing infrastructure than around static content delivery. These baselines should be codified, versioned, and revisited regularly as the architecture evolves.

Collaboration is just as important. Security automation cannot live in a silo. Developers, operations teams, and security engineers must align on what constitutes “secure enough” for various parts of the system. When security gates are seen as black boxes, they tend to get bypassed or resented. But when they’re viewed as part of a shared development culture, they become a foundation for trust. This cultural shift requires transparency engineers need to know why a deployment failed a check, how to fix it, and who to ask if they need to escalate. Clear documentation, traceable logs, and feedback mechanisms go a long way in reinforcing this mindset.

Scalability, too, is key. What works for a small team managing ten Terraform modules might break down when an enterprise is handling hundreds of microservices across regions. Automation pipelines must support modularity and separation of concerns. Different business units may need to manage their own policy sets, tied to their own risk profiles, while still conforming to a centralized security standard. Achieving this balance often involves building layered policy enforcement where some checks are local, and others are global and non-negotiable.

6.3 Case Study: Building Secure Automation at Scale in a Payment Ecosystem

In one of the more demanding projects I encountered, a regional payment gateway provider was preparing for a multi-country rollout across West Africa. Their platform handled everything from merchant onboarding to cross-border settlements, and the compliance requirements were steep. Each transaction had to meet varying local regulations for data protection, fraud monitoring, and system uptime. The challenge wasn't just scale; it was security at scale.

The organization had adopted cloud infrastructure early but was still managing much of it manually. Server provisioning, IAM updates, firewall changes, all of it passed through a combination of scripts and ticketing queues. As expansion plans accelerated, this setup began to crack. Environments drifted from one another, engineers made hotfixes without logging them, and security reviews lagged behind deployments.

The turning point came after a misconfigured network access control list (ACL) left a critical API exposed for nearly four hours. Although there was no breach, the near miss was enough to prompt a full overhaul of their infrastructure management strategy with automation and IaC at the core.

We began by rewriting their infrastructure templates using Terraform. Instead of ad hoc scripts, every resource compute instances, load balancers, storage, and IAM roles was defined declaratively. We established a clear folder structure separating production, staging, and dev configurations, with shared modules for baseline security controls: encryption standards, subnet isolation, and audit logging.

To avoid future lapses, we introduced automated security scans at two levels. First, every Terraform plan was scanned with tfsec before merging into the main branch. Second, once deployed, AWS Config continuously monitored live resources for violations triggering alerts if, for example, a security group was left open, or logging was disabled.

A version of policy library was also introduced. Instead of relying on engineers to "remember" what was secure, we codified rules: no plaintext secrets, all S3 buckets encrypted by default, no public IPs without explicit justification. These weren't just guidelines, they were enforced at the pipeline level using Sentinel, which blocked noncompliant deployments before they reached production.

The results were significant. Mean time to deployment dropped by 35%, not because steps were removed, but because decisions were standardized. Security incidents fell drastically, with misconfiguration reports declining by over 70% in three months. Perhaps most importantly, teams stopped seeing security automation as a bottleneck. It became part of their rhythm, a shared baseline that enabled them to build and iterate faster with confidence.

This case underscored a powerful truth: security automation isn't about slowing things down. When done well, it acts as a stabilizer keeping guardrails in place while allowing velocity. In high-stakes environments like payments, where both innovation and trust are non-negotiable, this balance is everything.

Chapter Seven

Identity Access Management and Zero Trust in Cloud Environments

In traditional on-premises systems, identity and access were often afterthoughts handled with broad roles, shared credentials, and assumptions that being inside the network implied trust. But in cloud-native environments, that model is not only obsolete, it's dangerous. The decentralization and scale of modern cloud ecosystems make identity the new security perimeter, and any assumptions of trust can open the door to catastrophic breaches.

One of the most common attack vectors in cloud systems today is privilege escalation. A user or service is granted far more access than it needs, often "just for testing," or because no one wants to block a release. That single over-permissioned role becomes a backdoor. And once an attacker or rogue process gets hold of it through leaked credentials, compromised keys, or social engineering, the damage is swift. From launching crypto mining operations to exfiltrating customer data, attackers no longer need to hack systems, they just log in.

The root of this vulnerability is not always a lack of controls, but a failure to enforce the **principle of least privilege**. Granting users only the exact permissions they need and no more is foundational to secure identity management. But enforcing this principle is challenging. Permissions evolve as teams grow, services change, and cloud providers introduce new features. Without constant review and refinement, what starts as a tightly scoped access policy can slowly bloat into a web of unchecked privilege.

These risks aren't hypothetical. High-profile breaches in recent years have traced back to misconfigured IAM roles, forgotten access tokens, and overly permissive policies that allowed attackers to move laterally across systems. These incidents reveal a painful truth: identity is the most powerful and most abused attack surface in the cloud.

That's why the paradigm shift is underway. Instead of assuming trust by default, organizations are moving toward **Zero Trust architectures**. In this model, no user, device, or workload is inherently trusted regardless of whether it sits inside or outside the network boundary. Every access request must be verified, validated, and continuously monitored.

Zero Trust isn't just a security strategy, it's a mindset. It means moving beyond perimeter-based thinking and designing systems under the assumption that breaches will happen. The goal is not to prevent all attacks, but to

minimize impact by ensuring attackers can't easily escalate privileges or access sensitive resources.

Implementing this mindset requires changes across people, process, and technology. It involves redefining access roles, segmenting networks, and embracing identity as a first-class security concern not a task left to backend teams after deployment. It requires visibility, automation, and ongoing scrutiny of who has access to what, and why.

7.1 The Evolution of IAM in the Cloud

The earliest days of cloud adoption were marked by convenience. Teams prioritized getting workloads online quickly, often at the expense of structured access control. It wasn't unusual for root credentials to be shared across teams or for engineers to use long-lived API keys stored in plaintext configuration files. These makeshift approaches worked until they didn't.

As cloud infrastructure grew in complexity, the need for secure, scalable, and auditable access mechanisms became impossible to ignore. Cloud providers responded by introducing more robust Identity and Access Management (IAM) services. These systems offered administrators fine-grained control over who could access what and under what conditions.

The introduction of **Role-Based Access Control (RBAC)** was one of the first major shifts. RBAC allowed organizations to define roles based on job functions like "Database Admin," "Developer," or "Auditor "and assign permissions to those roles, rather than to individual users. This reduced the risk of inconsistent privilege assignments and made access reviews more manageable. Instead of checking permissions user by user, teams could evaluate and update roles in a centralized way.

But RBAC had its limitations. In large organizations with complex workflows, roles often overlapped or became too broad. Engineers might be assigned to multiple roles simply to get the permissions they needed, leading to **privilege creep,** a slow, dangerous accumulation of excessive rights. Over time, these over-permissioned roles could be exploited, either unintentionally by internal actors or maliciously by attackers.

To address this, cloud platforms introduced **Attribute-Based Access Control (ABAC)** and **Policy-Based Access Control (PBAC)**. These models go beyond fixed roles and evaluate access based on dynamic attributes such as the user's department, project tag, geographic location, or time of day. For example, a policy could grant access to a storage bucket only if the request originates from a specific region and is tied to a particular service account.

This shift toward context-aware access brought significant improvements, especially in multi-tenant or distributed environments. It enabled teams to write more precise and adaptable policies, reducing the attack surface and tightening control without bottlenecking productivity. However, it also introduced a new complexity. Policies had to be meticulously crafted, monitored, and updated as infrastructure changed.

Amid this evolution, secrets management emerged as another crucial layer. Long-lived credentials and embedded tokens were replaced with **ephemeral credentials**, temporary tokens issued by secure identity services. These tokens expire quickly, reducing the window of opportunity for exploitation. Combined with secret managers like AWS Secrets Manager, HashiCorp Vault, or Azure Key Vault, teams could rotate credentials automatically and enforce strict access auditing.

Despite all these advancements, the success of IAM still hinges on visibility and discipline. It's one thing to have the technical ability to restrict accessit's another to consistently apply it across a sprawling infrastructure. That's why leading cloud organizations pair IAM tooling with **automated audits, anomaly detection, and regular access reviews** to ensure permissions stay aligned with business needs and do not silently expand.

Zero Trust is not a product. It's not a single tool or platform. Rather, it's a layered architecture guided by a single premise: never trust, always verify. In a cloud environment where applications, users, and devices interact across ephemeral, distributed systems, this mindset becomes not only relevant but essential.

The foundation of Zero Trust begins with **strict identity verification**. Every access attempt whether by a person, machine, or process must be authenticated using strong methods like multifactor authentication (MFA), federated identity providers, and certificate-based mutual TLS. Trust is earned moment by moment, never inherited from a static position in the network.

Next comes **least-privilege access enforcement**, the practical extension of identity verification. Even once authenticated, entities should only receive the minimum permissions necessary to perform a specific function. Instead of assigning broad privileges "just in case," access is scoped with precision and is time-bound where possible. Short-lived tokens, temporary credentials, and just-in-time access provisioning become the default.

Another critical component is **continuous context evaluation**. Traditional systems often authenticate once and assume trust persists. Zero Trust systems monitor behavioral signals continuously like geolocation anomalies, access frequency, device posture, and time of access and trigger re-evaluation or revocation if patterns shift. For example, a developer accessing a test environment from Lagos in the morning and then initiating a privileged change from Singapore two hours later should raise red flags.

Micro segmentation further strengthens Zero Trust architecture. Rather than allowing open communication within a cloud network, systems are divided into tightly controlled zones. Access between zones is granted explicitly, not implicitly. This limits lateral movement, containing breaches if they occur. Even if an attacker compromises one part of the system, they cannot automatically reach others.

In addition to segmentation, Zero Trust introduces **explicit access paths**. No one should access production systems from unmanaged devices or unsecured networks. Traffic should pass through secured gateways, often with identity-aware proxies or service meshes that enforce authentication and encryption at every hop.

Monitoring and visibility close the loop. Zero Trust environments require **centralized logging and real-time analytics** to ensure that identity verification and access enforcement are functioning as intended. Suspicious behavior is flagged early, and teams can trace actions back to a single identity or process whether human or automated.

Zero Trust is not achieved through one-time configuration. It's maintained through iteration. Policies must be regularly reviewed, tools tested, and assumptions challenged. This includes revisiting who has access to what, ensuring secrets are rotated, and verifying that identity providers are patched and up to date.

In practice, organizations rarely achieve Zero Trust overnight. It is a gradual migration starting with clear priorities, scoped projects, and measurable improvements. The journey of segmentation and hardening advances through access monitoring and segmentation and eventually touches everything from source control to third-party integrations.

7.2 Implementing Zero Trust with Major Cloud Providers

Adopting Zero Trust in cloud environments requires aligning architecture with both policy and platform capabilities. The three major cloud providers see; Microsoft Azure, and Google Cloud Platform (GCP)each offer extensive services that, when combined thoughtfully, allow organizations to implement Zero Trust principles across their infrastructure and applications.

On **AWS**, the building blocks begin with IAM roles and policies. AWS Identity and Access Management allows for precise role definition and the use of temporary security credentials through Security Token Service (STS), minimizing the risks tied to long-lived secrets. Pairing IAM with AWS Organizations enables centralized policy control across accounts, helping enforce security baselines at scale.

Network micro segmentation is achieved with **VPC Security Groups**, **Network ACLs**, and **Private Link** to restrict traffic to known endpoints. Zero Trust network access is further supported by **AWS Verified Access**, which replaces traditional VPNs by requiring device and identity verification before granting access to internal applications. Continuous evaluation can be embedded through **CloudWatch**, **AWS**

Config, and **Guard Duty**, enabling teams to detect anomalies and misconfigurations in real time.

On **Microsoft Azure**, Zero Trust is closely tied to Azure Active Directory (Azure AD), which functions as the central identity provider. Role-based access control (RBAC) integrates deeply with resource groups, subscriptions, and services, making fine-grained access control more manageable. Azure also offers **Privileged Identity Management (PIM)** to enforce just-in-time access and approval workflows for administrative roles ensuring that elevated privileges are used only when needed.

Network segmentation and identity-aware access can be built with **Azure Virtual Network**, **Network Security Groups**, and **Azure Firewall**. Azure's **Conditional Access Policies** bring context to authentication, factoring in risk signals, user roles, and device status to allow or deny access dynamically. Endpoint compliance, multi-factor authentication, and audit logging are consolidated through Microsoft Defender for Cloud, which surfaces policy violations and unusual behavior across the stack.

Google Cloud Platform (GCP) offers its own native interpretation of Zero Trust under the banner of **Beyond Corp Enterprise**. Instead of relying on network perimeter controls, Beyond Corp uses strong identity verification, device posture, and context-aware access to govern application reachability. **Cloud Identity** integrates with IAM policies to define what users and service accounts can do, while **VPC**

Service Controls and **Organization Policies** help prevent unauthorized data exfiltration.

GCP also supports just-in-time access through **Access Approval** and continuous security monitoring with **the Security Command Center**. Its **Context-Aware Access** engine uses signals such as IP address, location, device certificate, and group membership to determine access rights dynamically.

Despite the differences in implementation across providers, the underlying goal remains consistent: eliminate implicit trust, minimize privilege, and verify everything. Zero Trust implementation succeeds when teams architect flexibility, define access in code, and adopt secure defaults that make the safe path the easiest one.

A technology startup in the business analytics space was preparing for an enterprise expansion. Their SaaS platform hosted on a major cloud provider served dozens of clients, each with their own data partitions and user roles. As client onboarding accelerated, their leadership recognized a problem: the access model that had worked for a dozen clients couldn't support hundreds.

Each new tenant requires manual IAM configuration. The operations team rotated credentials manually. Developers had admin-level access to staging and production environments. Logs were siloed by service, and policy enforcement was inconsistent. The risk of privilege escalation, configuration drift, and cross-tenant exposure grew with every deployment.

The organization committed to a full security review and brought in external advisors to help refactor their cloud environment around Zero Trust principles. The process wasn't fast, but it was transformational.

First, the engineering and DevOps teams conducted a **permissions audit**, mapping every user, role, and service account against actual usage. The results were eye-opening. Over 70% of the assigned permissions were unused, and nearly 40% of service accounts had overlapping, conflicting privileges. Several short-lived development tools still had full access to production resources.

The next step was architectural. Each microservice was assigned its own identity, with clearly scoped roles enforced via the provider's IAM policies. Long-lived access keys were phased out in favor of temporary tokens issued by a secrets management tool integrated into the CI/CD pipeline. Services could now request credentials dynamically based on assigned trust levels, which were reviewed quarterly.

For customer data isolation, **resource-level policies and organizational boundaries** were introduced. This meant that even if a service failed, access was restricted by tenant boundary and role hierarchy. Logging was centralized, and identity-aware proxies were added in front of internal tools ensuring no one accessed production environments without strong identity verification and device posture checks.

On the user side, developers moved to just-in-time access for sensitive operations. Instead of holding standing access, they triggered short-term elevation requests that expired automatically. Audit logs captured who accessed what, when, and why with anomalies triggering Slack alerts and ticket reviews.

Culturally, the team embraced the **"verify first, access second"** mindset. Product managers participated in access reviews, security policies were added to sprint planning, and security debt was treated like technical debt tracked and prioritized. No more unchecked access. No more vague policies. Trust had to be earned every step of the way.

Six months after the transformation began, the company onboarded its largest enterprise client, a bank with strict compliance requirements. The client's security auditors found no high-risk findings during their cloud review. The startup passed the audit on the first attempt, gaining both credibility and confidence in its platform.

Chapter Eight

Securing APIs and Service-to-Service Communication

As organizations migrate from monolithic applications to microservices and distributed architectures, the role of the API has changed dramatically. APIs are no longer just back-end interfaces, they're front-line gatekeepers. In cloud-native environments, nearly every internal and external operation hinges on an API call: from data exchange and authentication to orchestration and analytics. With this central role comes heightened exposure and risk.

Unlike traditional systems protected behind a static firewall, cloud environments operate in a dynamic network where APIs serve as the new perimeter. This means that rather than protecting one single entry point, security teams must now secure thousands of touchpoints, each with their own access rules, data flows, and behavioral expectations.

Unfortunately, many APIs are deployed without adequate hardening. Default configurations, verbose error responses, overexposed endpoints, and lack of authentication mechanisms are still common. In environments where APIs are developed rapidly to meet business goals, security is often bolted on after deployment if at all.

The consequences can be severe. Public API leaks have exposed sensitive data ranging from payment records to health information. Internal APIs assumed to be safe because they're "not exposed to the internet" have been exploited through lateral movement after initial compromise. Insecure APIs don't just leak data; they undermine the trust model of the entire cloud architecture.

Recognizing this, cloud-native security has begun to treat APIs not as infrastructure side notes but as **first-class security assets**. That shift requires a change in how APIs are designed, deployed, and monitored. It begins with treating every API endpoint as potentially hostile regardless of its location in the network or its intended audience.

Effective API security starts with clear ownership. Development teams must be accountable for both the functionality and the defensibility of the APIs they build. This means defining what "normal" behavior looks like, understanding how data flows between services, and documenting intended use cases not just endpoints.

From there, security policies must be embedded directly into API design. Authentication and authorization are non-negotiable. Tokens must be short-lived and verifiable. Access should be scoped by role, service, or client application. And every response should be validated and sanitized to protect against injection or tampering.

But technical controls are only part of the equation. In the cloud, where services communicate at high frequency and scale, visibility becomes just as important. APIs must be observable not just monitored for uptime, but inspected for patterns, anomalies, and misuse. This means integrating logging, tracing, and rate-limiting mechanisms from the outset, so that security teams can respond quickly to emerging threats.

8.1 Authentication, Authorization, and the Cloud Token Economy

In a modern cloud architecture, the majority of security failures in API-driven applications aren't due to exotic zero-day exploits, they stem from weak or inconsistent authentication and authorization. These are the two pillars of control in an API-first ecosystem. Authentication verifies who or what is making a request. Authorization determines what that entity is allowed to do.

While the principles are straightforward, implementation across distributed systems is anything but. Services may use different languages, rely on different protocols, or exist in different regions. APIs may be accessed by humans, automated scripts, or third-party integrations. And with scale comes complexity: hundreds of services, each generating thousands of calls per second, with varied access rules and sensitivity levels.

To manage this, cloud systems have embraced **token-based authentication** as a universal translator. Rather than passing static credentials or passwords with each request, clients authenticate once typically with an identity provider and receive a token that encapsulates their claims. These tokens, often in the form of **JWTs (JSON Web Tokens)**, contain signed, verifiable information about the user or service making the request: identity, scope, expiration, and even contextual metadata like IP or device fingerprint.

Tokens allow for **stateless, distributed trust**. Services no longer need to query a central authority each time; they can independently verify a token's signature and extract its claims. This reduces latency and simplifies scaling. But it also introduces new challenges: token leakage, replay attacks, and the need for strict expiration and rotation policies.

To strengthen protection, cloud-native architectures often combine JWTs with **OAuth 2.0** or **OpenID Connect**. These frameworks separate the concern of issuing tokens from validating them. An identity provider (such as AWS Cognito, Azure AD, or Google Identity) handles user or client authentication and issues tokens according to predefined scopes. API gateways or services then validate those tokens before processing the request.

Even internal APIs benefit from this model. In service-to-service communication, machine identities authenticate using mutual TLS or workload identity systems. Tokens are issued programmatically, with time-bound access and fine-grained scopes. This not only limits the blast radius of a compromise but also ensures visibility into who is doing what, when, and from where.

Authorization, meanwhile, must move beyond static role mappings. Fine-grained access control is often implemented using **attribute-based access control (ABAC)** or **policy-based access control (PBAC)** allows decisions to be made dynamically, based on context: user attributes, time of day, resource sensitivity, or even compliance status.

In environments with layered APIs such as public APIs that are called internal microservices, this tiered authorization is vital. External clients may only access sanitized endpoints, while internal services require deeper privileges. Rate-limiting, throttling, and quota enforcement are layered on top to prevent abuse, whether intentional or accidental.

Misconfigurations in this layer are costly. A single overly permissive token or misapplied policy can expose entire datasets. That's why modern API authentication and authorization must be observable, testable, and tightly integrated into CI/CD pipelines.

While authentication and authorization define who can access an API and what they can do, equally important is securing the communication channel itself. In a distributed cloud environment, where services interact across regions, networks, and even providers, the potential for traffic interception, tampering, or impersonation is real. This is where **API gateways** and **mutual Transport Layer Security (mTLS)** come into focus.

An API gateway functions as the front door for service communication. It acts as a control point authenticating incoming requests, validating tokens, inspecting payloads, enforcing rate limits, and routing traffic to the appropriate backend. But more than just a traffic manager, it's a security sentinel. By consolidating these functions, it reduces the burden on individual services and standardizes protections across all exposed endpoints.

In practical terms, API gateways simplify Zero Trust implementation for external and internal APIs. Teams can define security policies once and apply them uniformly. Gateways also enable schema validation, input sanitation, and header inspection defenses against common threats like injection attacks, spoofing, and malformed requests. Logs generated by these gateways offer rich context for incident analysis and anomaly detection.

However, while API gateways secure the "front door," cloud-native systems often require **service-to-service encryption** behind the scenes. That's where **mutual TLS (mTLS)** comes in. Unlike standard TLS, which only verifies the server's identity, mTLS establishes trust in both directions. Each party, client and server must present a valid certificate, signed by a trusted authority, before the connection is allowed.

This is especially useful in multi-tenant environments, service meshes, and internal microservices where lateral movement is a concern. mTLS ensures that only verified services can speak to each other, even inside supposedly "trusted" networks. It also helps protect against **man-in-the-middle attacks**, particularly in environments with dynamic IPs or ephemeral workloads.

Major service meshes like **Istio**, **Linkerd**, and **Consul** use mTLS by default to encrypt east-west traffic between services. Certificates are rotated automatically, and policies can be enforced at scale ensuring that even fast changing microservice landscapes remain securely tethered.

In one deployment scenario, an organization enabled mTLS across hundreds of Kubernetes pods in their internal environment. Within days, they uncovered dormant services that were still transmitting plaintext data across zones bypassing security controls and exposing customer data in transit. The discovery prompted a full internal audit and the rollout of service identity enforcement, proving that visibility isn't a luxury in API security, it's a baseline.

8.2 Role of Schema Validation

Securing API endpoints and traffic is essential, but security doesn't end at the point of access. In cloud environments where API activity generates millions of requests per day, **observability** becomes an operational cornerstone. It's not enough to have logs; there must be intelligence behind the monitoring signals, not noise. Security teams need to see not just that a request was made, but what it contained, how it behaved, and whether it aligned with expected patterns.

This is where **real-time monitoring** and **behavioral analytics** become crucial. Platforms like AWS CloudWatch, Azure Monitor, Google Cloud's Operations Suite, or third-party tools like Datadog and Splunk allow teams to trace API calls end to end. But raw metrics alone aren't sufficient. To truly detect anomalies such as credential misuse, replay attacks, or privilege abuse, teams must combine telemetry with context.

Let's say a token is used to call an endpoint that a service has never accessed before, and it's coming from an unusual region. Alone, either event might be ignored. Together, they form a risk pattern. Modern observability tools are now built to ingest such telemetry, correlate it with metadata (like IP, device signature, or geolocation), and trigger alerts for unusual behavior.

API schema validation adds another layer of protection. Every API should have a clear schema that defines what inputs it accepts and what responses it returns. Enforcing these schemas at runtime prevents attackers from injecting malicious payloads, over posting data, or exploiting undocumented features. A strict contract acts as a guardrail if something doesn't match the expected pattern, it's dropped or flagged.

Moreover, schema enforcement can prevent subtle business logic abuse. For example, in e-commerce APIs, attackers may attempt to manipulate prices or bypass cart validation by injecting unexpected fields. A schema-aware gateway would detect and reject such requests before they reach the application layer.

To achieve this level of defense, APIs must be **versioned, documented, and tested** continuously. OpenAPI specifications (formerly Swagger) and GraphQL schemas are increasingly being paired with tools like Postman, Insomnia, and API validators to ensure consistency across development, staging, and production environments.

Finally, there's the human layer. Many threats emerge not because defenses fail, but because assumptions were made. A developer exposes a debug endpoint during testing and forgets to disable it. A QA token gets pushed to a public Git repository. A third-party integration is granted excessive scope for convenience.

Observability is what catches these gaps before they become breaches. Not just after the fact but proactively surfacing insights that help developers refine access rules, deprecate old endpoints, and adjust rate limits to balance usability and control.

8. 3 Case Study: When Internal APIs Go Public

A mid-sized digital services company operating in West Africa had recently undergone an ambitious re-architecture, migrating its monolithic back end into a modular microservices setup on a cloud-native platform. APIs became the connective tissue, linking payment processing, identity verification, notifications, customer service workflows, and more. Internally, the change was hailed as a success systems were faster, and deployment cycles had shortened dramatically.

But about six months into this new cloud-native journey, the company experienced a breach. Not through its user-facing application, but via an internal billing API. The endpoint had been exposed accidentally as part of a test environment left unsecured. It lacked rate limiting, proper authentication, and logging. Within days, an attacker discovered it and began scraping transaction metadata, extracting sensitive customer records from the cloud database.

What made the breach particularly dangerous was that the internal API was designed with trust in mind. Input validation was lax, responses were verbose, and the security team had deprioritized it because "it wasn't public." But in the cloud, internal no longer means isolation. The attacker pivoted through this entry point, gaining lateral access to services across the environment.

The incident forced the company into full crisis response mode. All API keys were rotated, affected customers were notified, and regulatory disclosures followed. Internally, it triggered a major review of the company's API architecture and assumptions. A cross-functional incident response team mapped every internal and external API and found several more endpoints without proper authentication or schema enforcement.

To rebuild trust, the company made three key changes:

- **Adoption of an API Gateway with mTLS and Centralized Policy Management** – This allowed all APIs, including internal ones, to be routed through a consistent security layer. Identity was verified for both users and services.

- **Schema Enforcement and Contract Testing** – API definitions were formalized and version-controlled. Any undocumented endpoints were deprecated or sandboxed. Runtime validation was enforced through API gateway rules.

- **Integration of Observability into CI/CD** – Developers could now push code only if test coverage included audit logging, access control validation, and schema compliance checks. Anomaly detection was enabled across key metrics like request spikes, unknown client origins, and unauthorized method calls.

More importantly, the cultural lesson was clear: **internal does not mean secure**. The perimeter has dissolved, and any service even one designed for backend processing must be treated as if exposed to the world. Trust must be earned at every hopping.

This case study echoes a broader trend across the cloud ecosystem. As systems become more modular and interconnected, APIs will remain a key attack vector and a key point of control. Security isn't just about protecting front doors anymore. It's about monitoring the hallways, locking side entrances, and logging every visitor, even the ones wearing employee badges.

Chapter Nine

Compliance Governance and Security Automation

Security teams would scramble to produce logs, sanitize environments, and draft documentation that reflected compliance more in theory than in practice. But in the cloud, that model simply doesn't scale.

The very nature of cloud infrastructure dynamic, ephemeral, and shared makes static compliance models obsolete. Resources spin up and down on demand. Identities shift across regions and roles. Data flows between services and platforms at speeds that outpaced manual reviews. And with increased reliance on automation, it's not just human error but misconfigured templates, CI/CD pipelines, and scripts that can introduce risk.

To address this complexity, cloud-native compliance must be **continuous, automated, and integrated**. It should not be something that slows down innovation. Instead, it should live alongside development, shaping behavior through guardrails rather than gates.

Modern governance begins with **understanding which frameworks apply**. For financial services, that might mean PCI DSS or ISO 27001. For healthcare, HIPAA. For organizations operating in Europe, GDPR sets the tone. And many companies, especially those working across borders or serving enterprise clients must adhere to multiple frameworks simultaneously.

This multi-framework environment demands more than awareness; it requires **architectural alignment**. A system designed without regard for auditability, data minimization, or breach notification timelines will struggle to retrofit compliance later. The most resilient organizations don't just "pass audits "they build systems that are inherently aligned with compliance expectations.

Cloud providers offer tools to support this. AWS has Config and Security Hub. Azure offers Defender and Policy. Google Cloud includes the Security Command Center. These services allow organizations to define **rules-as-code** policies that automatically check whether resources adhere to predefined standards. For instance, they can flag open S3 buckets, identify unencrypted databases, or block deployments that don't enforce MFA.

But tooling is only as effective as the **culture** that surrounds it. Compliance must be seen not as the job of one team, but as a shared responsibility. Developers must understand the implications of storing logs without retention policies. DevOps engineers must factor auditability into infrastructure templates. Business leaders must recognize that compliance risk is business risk.

When compliance becomes part of the development lifecycle not a stage after it, organizations gain more than just audit readiness. They gain clarity. They gain trust. And they gain the ability to detect and respond to deviations before they become violations.

One of the most transformative shifts in cloud security governance has been the rise of **Policy as Code (PaC)**a practice where compliance rules are written in machine-readable language and embedded directly into infrastructure pipelines. Instead of relying on static documentation or spreadsheets to track security requirements, organizations now define their policies as logic that can be evaluated, enforced, and audited automatically.

This approach changes the entire posture of compliance. It moves governance from reactive enforcement to **proactive assurance**. For example, instead of discovering after deployment that a cloud storage bucket is publicly accessible, a policy engine can block the deployment altogether until encryption and access controls are in place.

Languages and frameworks like **Open Policy Agent (OPA)** and **HashiCorp Sentinel** have enabled this paradigm shift. These tools integrate with cloud-native platforms, CI/CD pipelines, Kubernetes clusters, and infrastructure-as-code frameworks like Terraform. Policies can be used to enforce everything from tagging conventions and network boundaries to role definitions and encryption requirements.

What makes policy as code powerful isn't just automation, it's **visibility and consistency**. When rules are written once and applied everywhere, organizations reduce the risk of drift between environments. A developer deploying staging and production gets the same feedback loop. A compliance officer reviewing policy history sees not only what rules exist but when they are applied, who changed them, and how often they've been triggered.

Consider a cloud team managing hundreds of infrastructure deployments weekly. Without automation, it would be impossible to verify that each resource meets the same compliance standards. With PaC, every pull request triggers policy checks. Noncompliant code fails early, before anything reaches production. This early feedback improves developer awareness and reduces the need for late-stage remediation.

But PaC also introduces a new governance model; one that's **collaborative**. Security engineers write and maintain policy libraries. Platform teams integrate those policies into tooling. Developers review policy failures just like they review unit test failures. Instead of treating compliance as a wall, teams begin to see it as a **shared scaffolding** that supports faster, safer releases.

This collaboration extends to audit teams as well. Instead of requesting ad hoc screenshots or last-minute evidence during an external review, they can query policy logs, trace decisions, and demonstrate enforcement at scale. In a world of increasing regulatory complexity, that traceability isn't just helpful, it's essential.

Yet adopting a policy as code also requires discipline. Policies must be versioned, tested, and peer-reviewed just like any other part of the codebase. Poorly written or overly rigid policies can hinder delivery, erode trust, or introduce their own vulnerabilities. Governance must evolve from rigid control to **context-aware enforcement;** rules that adapt based on environment, risk profile, or business priority.

9.1 Continuous Compliance and Real-Time Auditing

As organizations move toward faster release cycles and ephemeral infrastructure, the idea of a once-a-year audit or quarterly compliance review becomes dangerously outdated. **Continuous compliance** is now the benchmark, an approach where systems constantly check themselves against predefined rules, flag deviations, and even correct them without human intervention.

This shift is made possible by a combination of **real-time monitoring**, **event-driven automation**, and **immutable infrastructure**. Instead of trying to inspect running systems manually, modern platforms collect logs, metrics, and configuration data in real time. These signals are analyzed continuously by compliance engines, which determine whether the environment adheres to policies around encryption, access control, data residency, and more.

For example, if a database instance is launched without encryption at rest, a compliance engine can do more than just alert, it can trigger a Lambda function or equivalent automation to shut it down, redeploy it with the correct settings, and notify the responsible team. This is not just detection, it's **self-healing** infrastructure.

Continuous compliance tools like AWS Config Rules, Azure Policy Compliance, and Google Cloud's Forseti Security allow organizations to build rule sets that cover the entire infrastructure lifecycle. These rules operate across accounts, regions, and services ensuring that governance is consistent even in complex, multi-cloud environments.

The benefits are profound. First, **audit fatigue** is reduced. Instead of conducting massive log pulls and system checks at the end of a cycle, organizations can simply export compliance reports from a dashboard that is always current. These reports include evidence: who made the change, what changed, when it happened, and whether it triggered a response.

Second, the **feedback loop tightens**. Developers and engineers are alerted to compliance issues the moment they arise not weeks later during a review. This real-time feedback leads to better decisions, fewer misconfigurations, and a stronger sense of ownership.

Third, **resilience improves**. Automated remediation ensures that even if mistakes occur and they always will the system doesn't stay vulnerable for long. Instead of relying on human reaction, compliance becomes part of the system's architecture.

However, achieving true continuous compliance also comes with challenges. Automation must be designed carefully to avoid false positives or unintended rollbacks. Teams must prioritize transparency, ensuring that enforcement actions are logged, explained, and reversible when necessary. And not every scenario can be handled automatically. Some controls, especially those involving third-party integrations or manual processes, still require human oversight.

Nonetheless, the direction is clear. Compliance is no longer a snapshot, it's a stream. And organizations that treat it as a living process gain not only audit readiness but also a stronger, more adaptive security posture.

9.2 Scaling Governance and Frameworks

As cloud environments grow in complexity across business units, regions, and even subsidiaries scaling governance becomes less about control and more about coordination. A single team can no longer oversee every workload or audit every deployment. Instead, security and compliance must be **delegated without being diluted**.

This is where governance frameworks and strategic team structures come into play. At the core is a principle that guides the most successful cloud programs: **centralized policy, decentralized execution**. In other words, the organization sets the standards but empowers each team to meet them using tools and processes suited to their context.

Frameworks like the **Cloud Adoption Framework (CAF)** from AWS, Microsoft's **Cloud Operating Model**, or Google's **Cloud Architecture Framework** all emphasize this approach. They encourage organizations to define shared principles such as encryption requirements, access controls, and resource tagging and implement them through reusable templates, policy libraries, and automated enforcement.

Guardrails are the mechanisms that make this possible. Unlike gates, which block progress until a condition is met, guardrails **guide teams within safe boundaries**. They can take the form of infrastructure blueprints, pre-approved CI/CD configurations, or account baselines that enforce compliance out of the box. When teams deviate, alerts are triggered but work doesn't necessarily stop. Instead, feedback loops are created, and learning is encouraged.

This approach requires strong collaboration between **platform teams**, who provide shared services and tools; **security and compliance teams**, who define the standards; and **product teams**, who build and ship solutions. Each group has a role, and governance only works when those roles are respected and clearly defined.

In many organizations, this is operationalized through a **Cloud Center of Excellence (CCoE)**a cross-functional team that provides templates, onboarding guidance, policy updates, and tooling support. Rather than acting as enforcers, CCoEs act as enablers. They don't block teams from moving fast, they **make it easier to move fast safely**.

Communication is also key. Compliance requirements must be written in plain language, mapped to technical controls, and embedded into documentation and training. Dashboards should provide visibility across environments, highlighting both strengths and risks. And reporting structures should enable transparency upward to executives and boards, so governance becomes a business function, not just a technical one.

As organizations scale globally or operate across regulatory environments, governance must also support **segmentation**. Policies may vary based on data sensitivity, user location, or business function. A one-size-fits-all model rarely works. Flexibility must be built into the governance design without compromising core principles.

Chapter Ten

Resilience Incident Response and the Future of Cloud Security

Cloud environments are often celebrated for their flexibility and scalability, but these strengths can obscure a deeper and more urgent concern: **resilience**. In a system where services are always changing, APIs evolve rapidly, and infrastructure spins up and down in minutes, the real test isn't whether a system can stay online forever, it's how quickly and gracefully it can recover when something goes wrong.

Resilience isn't about preventing failure altogether. In fact, cloud-native systems assume failure. Whether it's a zonal outage, a misconfiguration, or a supply chain vulnerability in an open-source dependency, something will eventually break. The goal is to design systems that can **withstand, isolate, and recover** from those failures with minimal disruption.

Architecting resilience begins with **redundancy**. Critical services should not be dependent on a single point of failure whether that's a region, a database instance, or a third-party integration. Instead, they should be distributed across availability zones, with failover mechanisms that allow traffic to reroute, storage to replicate, and workloads to shift dynamically.

Equally important is **observability**. Without visibility into system behavior, response times, and error patterns, teams can't respond effectively. Logging, metrics, and traces must be aggregated, centralized, and monitored in real time. More than that, they must be structured in a way that highlights anomalies, not just collects data. The sooner an issue is detected, the faster it can be contained.

Resilience also involves designing **graceful degradation**. If one part of a system fails, say, a recommendation engine or a reporting dashboard, it should not bring down the entire application. Instead, fallback mechanisms should be in place, allowing users to continue accessing core services while the non-critical component is restored.

One overlooked aspect of resilience is **dependency hygiene**. Many cloud systems rely on a web of open-source libraries, managed services, and third-party APIs. A vulnerability or downtime in any of these can cascade into serious issues. Regular auditing dependencies, strict version controls, and automated patching workflows are essential practices for maintaining integrity in the face of supply chain risk.

In cloud security, the ability to bounce back is just as important as the ability to stand firm. A resilient system does not simply protect itself; it protects user trust, operational continuity, and long-term business viability. And in a threat landscape that shifts as fast as the cloud itself, that resilience may be the most valuable defense of all.

10.1 Designing for Detection and Rapid Response

When incidents occur in cloud environments, speed matters. The gap between detection and response can determine whether a breach remains contained or escalates into a full-blown crisis. Modern cloud security, therefore, demands more than perimeter defenses, it requires a layered approach to **real-time detection** and **automated response orchestration**.

Effective detection starts with comprehensive visibility. It's no longer sufficient to monitor endpoints alone. In distributed systems, the attack surface spans containers, serverless functions, APIs, identity layers, and external integrations. Monitoring must encompass all layers from application and infrastructure logs to identity and access trails.

Security Information and Event Management (SIEM) platforms help consolidate these inputs, providing security teams with unified dashboards and actionable intelligence. But the real power lies in **correlation and context**. A single login from an unusual IP might not trigger alarms on its own but if it coincides with privilege escalation and outbound traffic spikes, it becomes part of a threat pattern. Cloud-native

SIEMs now leverage machine learning to surface these patterns and reduce alert fatigue.

Alongside SIEMs, **Extended Detection and Response (XDR)** tools and cloud-native solutions like AWS Guard Duty, Azure Defender, and Google Security Command Center offer integrated threat feeds and environment-specific recommendations. These tools contextualize risks based on real-time behavior and asset profiles, allowing teams to prioritize incidents based on impact.

Once a threat is detected, the next step is **containment**. Automated playbooks defined through Security Orchestration, Automation, and Response (SOAR) systems can trigger predefined actions like isolating a compromised workload, disabling credentials, or initiating forensic snapshots. These responses must be fast, transparent, and reversible when needed.

But automation alone doesn't replace human judgment. Incident response is ultimately a **human-driven process**, guided by structured protocols. That's why most mature organizations invest in **incident response runbooks** living documents that outline step-by-step procedures for triaging, escalating, and communicating during a crisis. These runbooks define roles, communication channels, legal considerations, and external disclosure requirements.

Practicing these protocols is just as important as writing them. Teams must conduct regular tabletop exercises and postmortems to validate assumptions and improve readiness. These exercises simulate real attacks, ransomware, data exposure, insider threats and challenge teams to respond under pressure.

Crucially, cloud environments require **cross-functional collaboration** during incidents. Security, operations, development, legal, and communications teams must coordinate seamlessly. Delays often stem not from technical limitations but from uncertainty who owns what, who approves which action, and how to communicate internally and externally.

Speed without clarity breeds chaos. But when detection systems are integrated, responsibilities are clear, and response actions are rehearsed, organizations can move with confidence even in crisis.

One of the most transformative shifts in cloud security culture is the embrace of **blameless post-incident reviews** structured reflections that prioritize learning over punishment. In complex systems, failure is inevitable. What determines long-term security maturity is how teams respond to failure, understand its causes, and implement lasting improvements.

A blameless postmortem does not seek to assign fault to individuals. Instead, it focuses on the conditions, systems, and decisions that allowed an incident to occur. This approach is rooted in psychological safety. When engineers and analysts know they won't be scapegoated, they are more likely to share critical details, surface mistakes honestly, and propose real fixes rather than political cover.

These reviews typically begin with a **timeline reconstruction**: what happened, when, and in what sequence. They examine logs, communications, escalations, and the behavior of both systems and people. This granular narrative helps uncover the true root causes, which are often far removed from the point of failure. A misconfigured security group, for example, might trace back to unclear onboarding documentation or an overprivileged template.

From there, teams ask "**how**" repeatedly rather than "**who**". How did the vulnerability get introduced? How did the alert fail to reach the right person? How did the system respond or fail to respond once the threat emerged? This iterative probing reveals systemic weaknesses rather than isolating human error.

The outcome of a postmortem is not just a report but a set of **actionable remediations**. These might include tighter controls, better tooling, updated runbooks, improved training, or changes to escalation paths. Importantly, these actions should be prioritized, tracked, and reviewed over time.

Postmortems lose value when they become a checkbox exercise rather than a catalyst for change.

Another crucial component is **knowledge sharing**. Lessons from an incident should not remain within the team that experienced it. Instead, they should be documented and disseminated across the organization via wikis, retrospectives, or briefings. This shared context builds collective resilience, allowing one team's learning to prevent future incidents elsewhere.

In high-performing organizations, postmortems even feed into **threat modeling** and **proactive defense planning**. If a pattern of incidents emerges around access control, that insight can inform the next sprint's security priorities. If an attacker exploited a known misconfiguration, teams could review how that vector is mitigated elsewhere. In this way, every incident becomes a source of threat intelligence.

Ultimately, the goal is not perfection but **adaptive security**. By analyzing incidents openly, responding systematically, and evolving continuously, organizations build systems and cultures that get stronger over time.

10.2 Case Study: Ransomware in the Cloud

In early 2022, a multinational logistics company faced a widespread ransomware incident that infiltrated their cloud-based operations platform. The attackers exploited a misconfigured storage bucket containing unencrypted credentials, which granted lateral access into critical workloads across multiple regions. In less than three hours, several containerized microservices were encrypted, and the customer-facing API layer went dark.

This case stands out not just because of the impact, it disrupted millions of shipments across four continents but because of the company's **measured, transparent, and ultimately successful** response. At the center of this recovery was a layered incident response plan that had been stress-tested in previous tabletop simulations.

From the moment anomalous traffic patterns were flagged, the internal Security Operations Center (SOC) activated a **multi-region isolation protocol**. All write operations to affected data layers were halted. Simultaneously, automated snapshots were taken of the compromised instances and stored in cold backup zones that were segmented from the main network.

The DevOps team quickly pivoted to a **clean infrastructure build**, using Infrastructure-as-Code templates that had been audited and versioned in advance. Within five hours, a read-only version of their platform was up, allowing customers to track existing shipments while business continuity teams coordinated alternative service routes.

What made this response particularly effective was the **clarity of roles**. The platform engineering team handled infrastructure rollback, the security team focused on attack analysis and containment, and the communications team issued real-time status updates internally and externally.

Executives were looped in every hour with status dashboards built into their incident management tooling.

After containment, the organization initiated a **full-scale forensic investigation**, in partnership with external cybersecurity firms. They traced the root cause to a former test environment that had been accidentally promoted to production during a rush deployment two months earlier. It lacked endpoint detection, access logging, and storage encryption.

In the weeks that followed, the company didn't just recover, they emerged stronger. They launched a **zero-trust redesign** of all access layers, implemented mandatory runtime encryption, and enforced stricter identity federation policies across their development teams. More notably, they published a detailed post-incident report publicly, outlining the breach, the lessons learned, and the roadmap for reform.

That decision to be transparent earned them more customer trust not less. In fact, within three months, survey feedback showed customer confidence in their security had increased.

This case demonstrates a fundamental truth in cloud security: resilience is not just a function of tooling or technical architecture. It's also about **leadership, preparation, and accountability**. When all three are present, even the most severe disruptions can be contained and even transformed into an opportunity to lead by example.

In this emerging landscape, **AI-powered defense** will shift from detection to anticipation. Behavioral analytics, trained on vast telemetry data, will not only flag anomalies but forecast potential breaches based on pattern divergence and risk modeling. These systems will act not just as alert engines, but as adaptive agents adjusting access privileges, throttling traffic, or sandboxing code before malicious activity unfolds.

Alongside this, **policy-as-code** will become the default. Rather than relying on human memory or periodic checklists, compliance and governance will be baked directly into infrastructure definitions. These policies will evolve through version control like any software artifact, reviewed, tested, and rolled out across environments without ambiguity.

Security teams will also need to adapt to an **API-first, composable infrastructure model**, where services are modular and interconnected. This architectural shift demands deep visibility across the dependency graph. The weakest link is it a third-party function, an open-source library, or a misconfigured webhook that can expose the entire system. Tools that map and monitor these relationships in real time will become as essential as firewalls once were.

Moreover, as **multi-cloud and hybrid architectures** become the norm, portability of both workloads and security standards will be critical. Organizations must ensure that their protections travel with their assets whether they're deployed on AWS, Azure, GCP, or at the edge. Identity will serve as the unifying layer, and federated access controls will play a pivotal role in maintaining consistency across disparate platforms.

But technology is only part of the equation. The next era of cloud security also requires a shift in how we train, hire, and lead. Security must be democratized, understood by developers, embedded in product decisions, and championed by leadership. The strongest defense will come not from a siloed security department but from **a culture of continuous awareness, shared responsibility, and institutional memory**.

The threats will evolve. New vulnerabilities will emerge. But the principles that undergird secure systems resilience, transparency, and intentionality will remain. What changes is how those principles are executed on a scale.

Reviews

1. Dr. Femi Adigun

Chief Information Security Officer, Lagos FinServe

"Mariam Sanusi has written the kind of book we desperately need in today's cloud-first world, one that doesn't just dwell on theory but offers practical, lived experience. Her emphasis on DevSecOps and automation is spot-on. This book is already mandatory reading for my engineering and security teams."

2. Ezinne Okoye

Lecturer, Cybersecurity & Cloud Architecture, University of Nigeria, Nsukka

"What sets Cloud-Driven Defense apart is how it bridges technical depth with clarity. Mariam explains complex cloud principles without losing the nuance professionals require. As someone training the next generation of cloud security experts, I find this book incredibly useful both as a reference and a teaching tool."

3. Dipo Hassan

CTO, KoraPay Nigeria

"We operate in high-stakes environments where cloud resilience is non-negotiable. Mariam gets that. Her insights on secure development pipelines, IAM, and governance reflect what real

startups face every day. This isn't just a book; it's a mirror to the challenges cloud-first teams face in Africa and beyond."

4. Aminat Sulaiman

Cloud Solutions Architect, Abuja Techworks

"I've followed Mariam's work for years, and this book captures everything that makes her approach unique, deeply technical, always grounded in real-world problems, and never losing sight of the people behind the systems. This will be a staple in many cloud teams across Nigeria."

5. Uche Chinedu

Head of IT Risk & Compliance, Zenith Capital

"Reading this book felt like having an expert consultant walk me through a complete secure cloud transformation, from infrastructure design to post-deployment monitoring. It's refreshing to see a Nigerian cybersecurity voice take on the global cloud conversation with such authority."

References

- *Anderson, R. J. (2020). Security engineering: A guide to building dependable distributed systems (3rd ed.). Wiley.*
- *Arora, A., & Garg, A. (2021). Hands-On Cybersecurity with Blockchain: Implement decentralized security models with blockchain. Packt Publishing.*
- *Babcock, C. (2022). Cloud computing: Proven methods to ensure data security. Springer.*
- *Chen, L. Y., & Zhang, Y. (2021). Cloud security and privacy: Challenges and solutions. Journal of Cloud Computing, 10(1), 1–15.* https://doi.org/10.1186/s13677-021-00252-8
- *Microsoft. (2022). Zero Trust Security Model. Microsoft Learn.* https://learn.microsoft.com/en-us/security/zero-trust/
- *Google Cloud. (2023). Security foundations blueprint.* https://cloud.google.com/architecture/security-foundations
- *Fitzgerald, J., & Dennis, M. (2020). Cyber resilience: A guide to building a secure and resilient organization. CRC Press.*
- *Kim, D., & Solomon, M. G. (2021). Fundamentals of information systems security (4th ed.). Jones & Bartlett Learning.*

- *McShane, J., & Baxter, A. (2021). Practical cloud security: A guide for secure design and deployment. O'Reilly Media.*

- *OWASP Foundation. (2023). OWASP Top Ten for Cloud-Native Applications.* https://owasp.org

- *National Institute of Standards and Technology (NIST). (2020). NIST Special Publication 800-53 Rev. 5: Security and privacy controls for information systems and organizations.* https://csrc.nist.gov/publications/detail/sp/800-53/rev-5/final

- *Sharma, S. (2022). DevSecOps: A leader's guide to producing secure software without compromising flow, feedback, and continuous improvement. IT Revolution Press.*

- *Ristenpart, T., & Yilek, S. (2021). Cloud computing security: Past, present, and future. Communications of the ACM, 64(5), 30–32.* https://doi.org/10.1145/3447772

- *Threat Modeling Manifesto. (2020). A manifesto for threat modeling.* https://www.threatmodelingmanifesto.org/

www.ingramcontent.com/pod-product-compliance
Lightning Source LLC
LaVergne TN
LVHW101503200926
848483LV00001B/212
* 9 7 8 2 3 5 4 4 1 2 7 1 5 *